typical 10x10

Add-ons near checkout

Banasree

SUCCESSFUL BAKERY DESIGN

Edited by Vanessa Cullen

DESIGN MEDIA PUBLISHING LIMITED

Editor's words

The oven of former bakery often directly faces to the street, and you stand a good chance to run into the baker who was carrying a bake tray. Then you bought bread while making way for the baker. This suddenness might bring you constraint feeling, instead of the joy of tasting. At that time, the bakery had its own advantage for providing delicious food and paid no attention to the design of the bakery itself.

However, we are now living in an age that pursues full-sensory experience. The bakery operators begin to lay the same emphasis on the general design of space as on the flavour of the baked products, from creating a specific atmosphere to a detailed furnishing, from visual enjoyment to smelling and taste. Bakery is no longer a place to step in for a piece of bread and then leave in hurry; it is an attracting space for you to pick out delicious food and then enjoy. It is warm, romantic, and sweet; it can showcase the history of bread or the spirit of baker; it can share with you the story of the delicious bread.

Designers often take the colour and flavour of bread into account when designing a bakery and transfer them into visual elements. It is important to create a space that can attract customers when they first step in and can evoke their desire to buy. That is what designers and the bakery operators should consider.

Contents

008 *Chapter 1: Overview*

010 Evolution of Baking Industry in Europe

010 European Baking Market

012 Characteristics of Baking industry in China

013 Current Performance

013 Industry Outlook

014 Baking Industry Analysis

015 Internal Rivalry

015 Barriers to Entry

015 Distributors

015 Suppliers

016 Substitutes

016 Components of Bakery

016 Labour

016 Machinery

017 Government Regulations

017 Product

Handwritten notes (left side):

Product Mix Base
Breads: White, Milk, Low GI, Burgers, Crusty
Puffs & Zesty, Low GI, Cronuts, Spiral
Savoury: Pizza Bun, Pizzas
Sandwichs: Chicken, Peppery, Bolein
Cakes, Butter&Fruit, Chocolate
Cookies: Crusty&disk, moist
Celebrating Cakes: Vanilla, Coffee, Blackforest, Tiramisu

Reference I Like
1 Page 068, Colored chairs
2 Page 098, Display
3 Page 128
4 Page 140
5 Page 180
6 Page 182

---

018 **Chapter 2: *Preparation***

020 **Relative Instructions**

022 **Site Selection** — School, office, commercial, community.

022 Capital Cost

022 Passenger Flow

023 Rivalry Elements

023 Target Customers

023 Transportation Factor

030 **Chapter 3: *Holistic Design***

038 **Branding** — MTI notes
Dawn's 4C#: Connection, Craving, Celebrating, ...

038 Be Specific about the Target Market

039 Create a Positive Perception of the Brand Name

039 Brand Consistency

039 Deliver on What the Brand Promises

039 POS Materials Help Leave an Imprint of the Brand

040 Sell Branded Retail Merchandise — Cupcake Stand, Tshirt, Mug, Birthday candle, toppers

042 **Shopfront Design**

042 Theme — Rustic, Chalk BlackBoard, Urban traditional elements, contemporary, varity colour Eubstool & chair, raw wood, Iron

Contents

042 Symbol

042 Unity

043 Diversity

043 Specificity

050 **Interior Design**

052 Interior Layout

100 Colour & Graphic Design

100 Materials

188 **Economical Ways to Update Existing Bakery**

188 Freshen Up with Paint

188 Hang Wallpaper

188 Use Mirrors

188 Paint the Floors

189 Get New Fabric

189 Look for Second-hand Options

189 Be Creative with Props

189 Work with Artists on Consignment

191 Chapter 4: Display

192 **Client's Demands**

192 **Display Case**

192 Refrigeration

192 Lighting

193 Air Circulation

212 **Tips to Improve Displays**

216 Chapter 5: Design Guidelines and Standards

218 **Premises, Equipment and Vehicles**

212 **Furniture, Utensils and Floor**

219 **Cleanliness and Sanitation**

219 **Sitting or Lounging Equipment**

219 **Lighting and Safety Lighting**

220 **Wearing Apparel**

220 **Keeping and Handling of Products and Ingredients**

220 **Use of Ingredients**

221 **Smoking**

222 Index

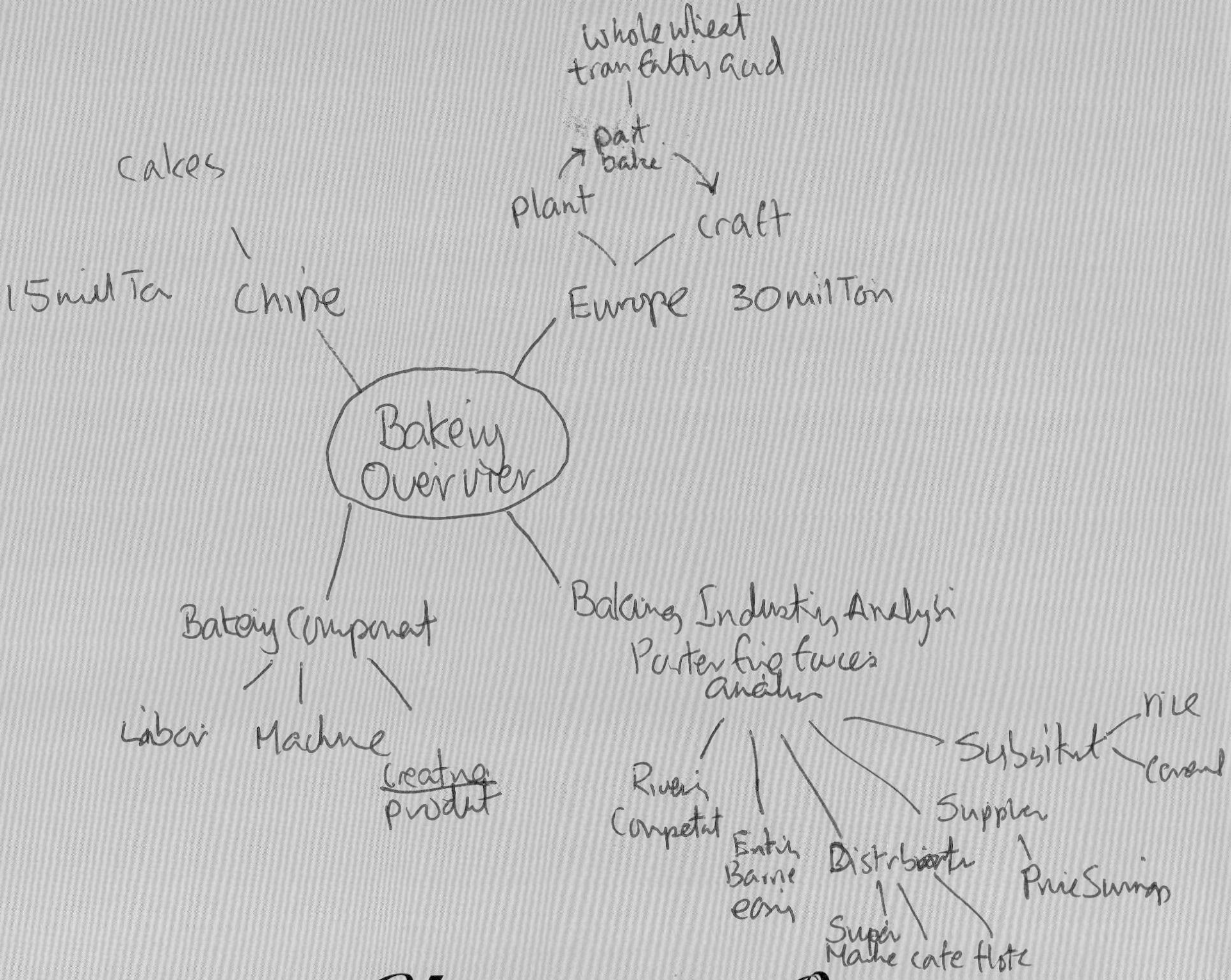

Handwritten mind map:

- **Bakery Overview** (center)
  - cakes / China — 15 mil Ton
  - Europe — 30 mil Ton
    - plant → par bake → craft
    - whole wheat, trans fatty acid
  - Bakery Component
    - Labor
    - Machine
    - Creating Product
  - Baking Industry Analysis — Porter five forces
    - Rivals / Competition
    - Entry Barriers easy
    - Distributors — Super Market, cafe, hotel
    - Suppliers — Price Swing
    - Substitutes — rice, cereal

Chapter 1: Overview

1. Evolution of Baking Industry in Europe

2. Characteristics of Baking Industry in China

3. Baking Industry Analysis

4. Components of Bakery

Chapter 1: *Overview*

1. Evolution of Baking Industry in Europe

Europe is the cradleland of western-style pastry which has had a long history and gained great achievement in countries such as UK, France, Spain, Germany, Italy, Austria, Russia and so on. As regards to the development of western-style pastry, bread enjoys the longest history. In the 4th century, there was a professional bakery association in Rome. In the Renaissance period, the western-style pastry began to be endowed with modern features both in form and production method. Bakery industry has become an independent industry and stepped into a new and prosperous era from then on. (Figure 1-2)

In the 18th and 19th centuries, the western bakery industry entered a new stage under the impact of reform in government system, natural science and industrial revolution. Meanwhile, the baking method evolved from household making into industrial production and formed a complete system. In the Victorian Age, western-style pastry came into a flourishing period. At present, the bakery industry is rather developed in European and American countries and becomes an important pillar in food service industry.

European Baking Market
A study from the European Commission found that in 2010 the European bread consumption was around 32 million tonnes in the EU 27 countries. Across the whole of the European countries the market share of the industrial bakers vs. the craft bakers was approximately 50%:50% but there were great differences in different countries. The total consumption of bread, viennoisserie and patisserie was estimated as nearly 39 million tonnes in the EU 27 countries. Bread production is relatively stable in most countries but there are some countries which are still showing a long term trend of a slow decline, 1%-2% per year, including the United Kingdom and Germany. Bread consumption patterns differ widely within the EU but most countries have an average consumption of 50 kg of bread

Figure 1-2. Craft bakery shop

per person per year.

Table 1: Market share of plant and craft bakeries (% turnover)

Country	Plant Bakeries	Craft Bakeries	Others
Austria	20.0	80.0	
Belgium	36.1	58.8	5.1
Denmark	51.0	49.0	
France	23.0	68.0	9.0
Germany	35.0	65.0	
Italy	10.0	90.0	
The Netherlands	73.7	21.0	5.3
Spain	34.0	66.0	
United Kingdom	80.0	3.0	17.0

From Table 1, it can be understood that the craft bakeries are still very popular in most European countries.

One area of continued growth throughout Europe is the market demand for frozen dough and part-baked products which has transformed the market so that co-operatives and industrial baking companies are flourishing at the expense of the craft sector. In-store bakeries continue to be a growing sector. There also continues to be increased demand for greater variety of bread than conventional breads. Bread with oats, bran and seeds are very popular in the UK. There is also a growing trend for increased production of sliced and wrapped bread in many countries across Europe including Germany and France. There will be continued growth in morning goods and specialty breads with lots of opportunities for innovation.

With growing trend calling for product innovation and health food, whole wheat, fiber and unsaturated fatty acids made an important contribution. There will be a continued decrease in bread consumption as alternative foods and bakery type products are increasingly available. Consumers are interested in natural experience, convenience and indulgence and growing out of home consumption meaning less time spent on home food preparation and consumption.

2. Characteristics of Baking Industry in China

With the improvement of living conditions in China, the dietary structure changes a lot as well. In order to satisfy people's demand for new types of pastries, the bakery market presents an unprecedented prosperous picture in China.

Bakery industry in China plays a significant part in food processing industry, and has developed rapidly during the past yeas. The developing trend of biscuit making, bread making and pastry making involved are being diversified. The biscuit industry is characterised by a comparatively mature market with a highly modernised and outstanding processing in large scale, while the bread making industry features a combination of processing of large scale and specialisation. As a typical traditional product, cake is regarded as a festal food closely related with culture and etiquette, and its making method has been developed a lot through innovative techniques and ideas. As regards of cakes, Western pastry making enjoys rapid development in China in recent years.

Current Performance
Bakery output increased from 429,300 tons in 2005 to 15,000,000 tons in 2010, representing annualized growth of 28.5%. In 2011, bakery output is expected to increase by 21.5% to 1.83 million tons. Relatively low entry barriers and high profitability attracted many new entrants to the industry over the past five years, which contributed to increased output. Revenue is expected to increase by an annualized rate of 26.6% over the five years through 2011, with an 18.1% increase to $7.45 billion in 2011.

Industry Outlook
The industry is expected to maintain positive growth in the next five years. Revenue is forecast to increase by an annualized 11.6% to reach $12.91 billion in 2016. This growth will be driven by favorable domestic demand for bread and bakery products as household disposable incomes rise. However, as the industry matures, growth will be slower than the high levels of the past five years. As output volumes slow, increased competition will result in lower prices for bread and bakery products. Revenue is forecast to grow by only 8.4% in 2016.

In terms of the overall development status of bakery industry, there is still a great distance to the foreign bakery industry, such as the large gap with respect to technical matters and equipments when compared with those of international producer; the low degree of specialty of material, lack of subdivision of material and of technology; the lack of research workers and skilled workers. So far as the bakery industry is concerned, innovation, safety, nutrition, convenience and dainty are needed for its develop-

Chapter 1: *Overview*

Figure 3-4. Various baked products

[handwritten: what is Porter's Five Forces analyse]

ment. The dedicated equipments, material will experience an outstanding progress, and the trend of development will be processing in large scale, and chain operation. Besides, bakery industry in China in the following years will experience a rapid growth, more fierce competition and it will be facing a large market space. (Figure 3-4)

3. Baking Industry Analysis

Porter's Five Forces analysis is useful when trying to understand the competitive environment facing a given industry. It involves looking at internal competition, barriers to entry, the profit-appropriating power of both buyers and sellers, as well as substitutes to the goods produced. Applied to the bakery industry it shows an average net profit that typically does not cover the cost of capital due to low barriers to entry, ease of production and ease of access to ingredients.

Internal Rivalry
There are many players in the bakery industry. The top four companies are estimated to only account for 11.7 percent of the market. The industry is characterised by small bakeries, but there has been a recent trend towards consolidation and economies of scale. Businesses compete on price, quality, differentiation and relationships with key suppliers.

Barriers to Entry
Barriers to entry in this industry are low. Economies of scale are beneficial, but not required for industry success. As a result, small businesses can enter the industry with a relatively small amount of capital. The two main determinants of a new company's success is the leaders' ability to acquire sufficient distribution channels to cover operating costs and their ability to build up brand recognition and loyalty. Distribution channels typically involve retail outlets, such as supermarkets and grocery stores, and they can be more easily acquired if the bakery has an established brand or the marketing resources to create one.

Distributors
Distributors of the bakery industry's products, such as supermarkets, grocery stores, hotel chains and convenience stores, are able to appropriate much of the industry's profit due to the large number of small bakeries that are all vying to find outlets for their products. As a result, distributors are able to command low prices and volume discounts. Only large players, such as Kraft, Kellogg, Yamazaki Baking and Grupo Bimbo, have the power to level the playing field and achieve a more balanced share of the profits.

Suppliers
Suppliers do not have much negotiating power in the bakery business due to the well developed markets for their products and the commoditized nature of what they are selling. Bakeries can be affected by price swings of the raw inputs, but the changes are a result of global supply and de-

Chapter 1: Overview

Figure 5-6. Baked products

mand determinants rather than suppliers' negotiating power.

Substitutes

Many substitutes exist for bakery products. Breakfast cereals, rice and potatoes are all viable alternatives and individuals can also make all of the baked goods they want at home. Bakeries rely upon price and convenience to keep individuals switching to a substitute or baking what they need at home.

4. Components of Bakery

Bakeries around the globe bake bread and create cakes, muffins and other desserts. Large bakeries use machines for production while smaller bakeries work with smaller equipment. The components or basic elements and ingredients of the bakery industry cover the entire parameters of small and large bakeries worldwide.

Labour

Labour comprises one of the key components of the bakery industry. Larger plants run mostly through automated production equipment, but workers need to oversee the management, quality and output of the machines. Bimbo Bakeries, USA, the largest bakery in the nation, operates 35 bakeries and mans over 7,000 routes.

Machinery

The machines of the baking industry comprise another major component. Every bakery, no matter the size, needs ovens to bake the bread. Other necessary machines and equipments for smaller bakeries include sifters, slicers, molds, freestanding and electric mixers, a variety of refrigerators and cooling equipment, and all types of kitchen tools. Larger bakeries use dough proofing machines, large scale mixers, machines to roll out or shape dough and huge ovens.

Government Regulations

The bakery industry must comply with all types of federal regulations regarding food, which vary from state to state. States address such details as the cleanliness of floors, walls and ceilings; the state of the vehicles used to transport bakery products and the storage of ingredients. Other considerations include furniture and utensil sanitation, staff clothing, smoking policies, hand washing procedures, the proximity of animals and licensing. Government regulations also address the vitamin enrichment of bread, including thiamine, riboflavin and niacin.

Product

While bread may be the mainstay of the baking industry, shows such as 'Ace of Cakes' and 'Cake Boss' have extolled the virtues of creativity in the market. Whether it's a new flavour of an already existing product or a completely new dessert creation, producing quality items is a major process in the baking industry. (Figure 5-6)

Creative Product

017

Chapter 2: Preparation

1. Relative Instructions

2. Site Selection

Chapter 2: *Preparation*

1. Relative Instructions

Identify one's vision for the bakery by creating a life plan that incorporates passion and how a bakery fits into one's life goals. Defining what one expects from the bakery also helps when it's time to write the business plan. List positives and negatives involved in starting a bakery to see if the pros outweigh the cons.

Decide whether to start from scratch, purchase a bakery franchise or buy an existing bakery. Possible franchises include cafés such as Panera Bread, a donut shop such as Krispy Kreme or specialty pastries such as Cinnabon. Buying a bakery is the quickest way to become a bakery owner, but be cautious as to why the owner wants to sell.

Research the community where one plans to locate the bakery in terms of need for a bakery, whether there are enough customers, if there is a convenient location, what products the market wants and if you can provide superior customer service.

Obtain financial support to start the bakery. Different sources of financial support include personal credit cards, savings, personal investments, a bank loan, venture capitalists, government grants, small business loans, loans or gifts from family or an investment by an individual who is successful in the field.

Conduct pre-opening activities such as obtaining any necessary licenses, permits and insurance. Open a bank account, contract suppliers, set up utilities, purchase equipment and hire and train employees. Organize these duties and hire individuals that have an expertise in these areas if needed. Keep track of the tasks and their progress in an organizer or spreadsheet.

Generate interest in the bakery before opening by putting up a sign as soon as possible and promoting the grand opening date. Get business cards early and hand out whenever possible to generate interest. (Table 2)

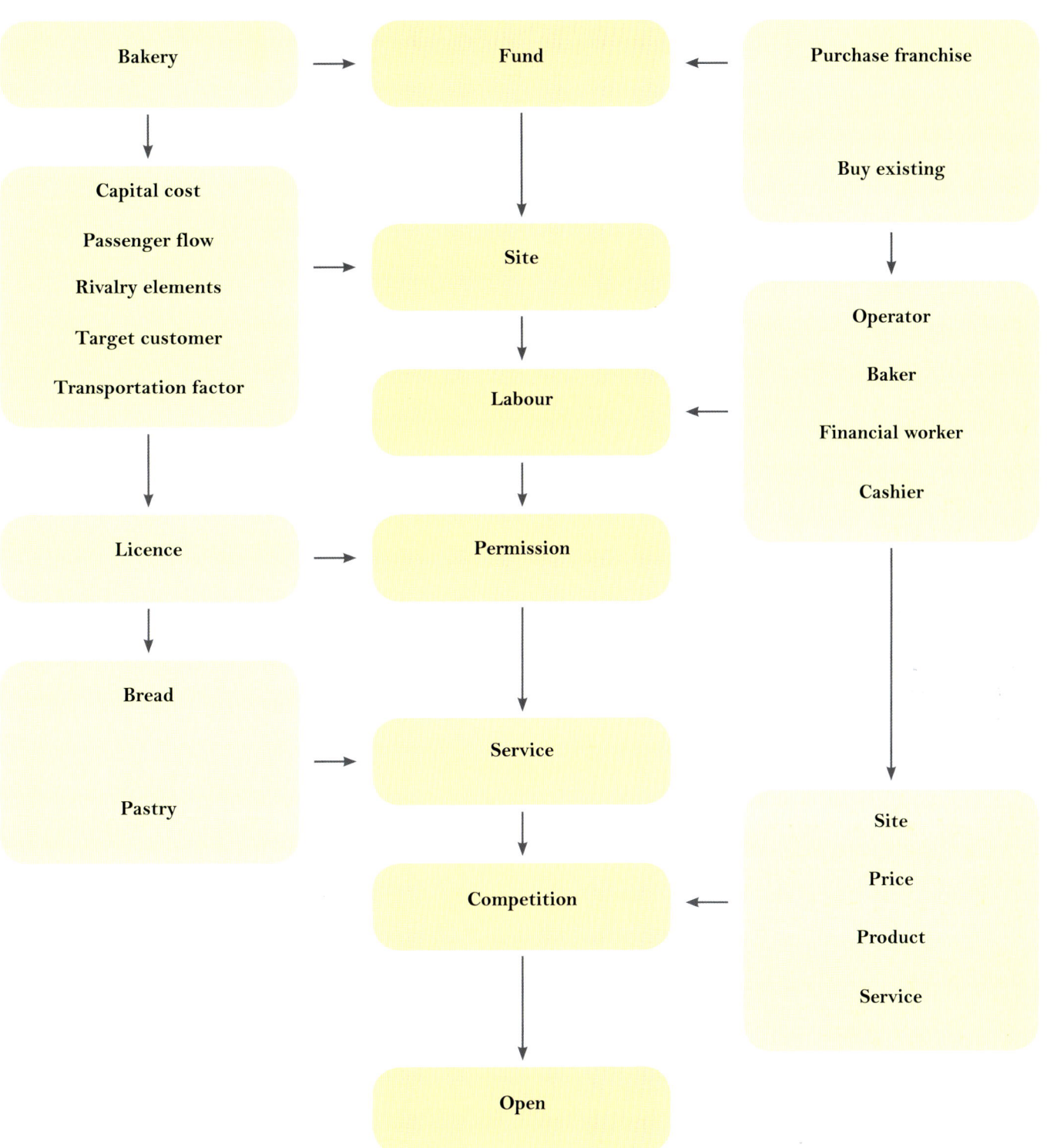

Above: Table 2

Chapter 2: Preparation

2. Site Selection

Site selection is usually an important and difficult step for the success of the Bakery. For a bakery, site selection has its own characteristics. People in the industry believe 'site selection determines the success of a specific bakery'. A favorable operating environment is essential for a thriving business, but how to evaluate the business environment is rather complicated. For example, a small bakery hidden deep under a street is packed with customers nearly every day, while a big bakery facing a busy street sits mournfully empty almost each day. To create a favorable business environment, the operator must have a complete understanding of the surrounding business circle. In the business circle, it means the scope of operation a site can cover with bakery as the central point. Being estimated, the following five elements can be taken into account.

Capital Cost
A small craft bakery with rapid turnover of products needs to be sited in a prime area, which requires a relatively high rent; a plant bakery which always requires more space can be located in an area with relatively low rent.

Passenger Flow
Usually, a bakery needs to be located in an area with high passenger flows to provide convenience to potential customers. Customers of a bakery can be divided into three types: those specially fond of products of the bakery, those shared with adjacent bakeries and those just dropping by. The passenger volume is almost the same in different areas, but it still needs specific analysis for the differences in purpose, speed and staying time. In the common area, it is commuting time that the passenger flow achieves the highest point, while in the downtown or night fair, it is off-working time or night time that welcomes more customers.

Rivalry Elements

In a certain business circle, the more the bakeries there are, the more fierce the competition. In usual, there are several elements that affect the purchasing behaviour of customers. However, there is no doubt that excessive amount of bakeries can separate the customers.

Target customers

There often are great differences towards bakery products among different customers. Generally speaking, the number of target customers in a specific area is relatively fixed regardless of the mobile population. A survey shows that the state of operation varies with time in different areas. In office area, it is blooming in commuting time; in the business area, it is prosperous all day; in the area with schools, it is flourishing in school hours.

Transportation Factor

If a bakery is located in an area where the traffic is convenient, it is rather beneficial for the development of it. Analysis of distance and direction towards bus station or quay for bakeries on the edge of business centre is required. For example, if a bakery is located opposite the bus station, then the potential customers are alighting passengers, while if a bakery is sited adjacent to the bus station, then the target customers are boarding passengers. Additionally, the parking facilities can be designed according to the size of business circle, location and scale of a bakery, adjacent parking lot, vehicle amount of non-purchasers and vehicle amount in different periods.

Summarising from the above analysis, the following environments are recommended for bakeries:
(1) Specific location in business area;
(2) Hub of communications with high passenger flow;
(3) Areas with more schools;
(4) Residential community.

Chapter 2: *Preparation*

Vyta – Boulangerie Italiana

Designer: Marco Lombardini,
Marco Capponi/Colli+Galliano Architetti
Location: Rome, Italy
Project area: 150m²
Project year: 2008
Photographs: Matteo Piazza

The project developed from one of the most simple and antique components on our dining table – bread. This bakery was created inside a railway station, the modern symbol of speed and progress.

The precise desire for integration and dialogue with the architectonic context is obvious from the very beginning. It shows that Vyta is totally projected towards the outside, and separated from it by a simple black portal. This was the theme of the interior design for the bakery, which starts from the traditional image of the bread shop; this is then reduced progressively to its essential features, in the quest for immediate and universal language, that can guarantee the maximum usability in this place of transition.

The familiar colours of oak wood harmonise with the pale colours of the flooring and the ceiling, leaving space for monolithic furnishing accessories in black Corian that catalyse the attention through their symbolic purity. The polyfunctional counter is the heartbeat of every busy shop and in this case is used as an essential exhibition structure. There is a large decorative wall consisting of a paste creation symbolising the surface and the fragrance of a bread crust. This element has strong aesthetic and metaphoric connections and is used as the backdrop to a series of elongated tables and benches, where the consumption of a hasty meal is mixed with the ancient ritual of conviviality thanks to the intelligent use of lighting, enhanced by spherical suspension lamps in chrome-plated metal that invite and beckon while amplifying the space.

In a delicate combination of prospects, the counter and the wall behind it curve towards the more intimate portion of the room, animated by tables and chairs submerged in a welcoming atmosphere and display alcoves similar to compact black boxes. These offer wines and oils originating from various regions in Italy. There is maximum design uniformity that slides unobtrusively into the busy station, while allocating ample room for the people waiting to depart, creating a relaxing ambience closely linked to the traditions that are hidden behind the minimalist lines – making Vyta a valid alternative to fast food, and promoting good food culture.

1. Vyta Bakery was created inside a railway station, the modern symbol of speed and progress. The precise desire for integration and dialogue with the architectonic context is obvious from the very beginning. It shows that Vyta is totally projected towards the outside, and separated from it by a simple black portal.

VyTA
BOULANGERIE

La Natura offre
elementi semplici:
acqua, grano e fuoco.
La mano esperta,
la pazienza
e la creatività dell'uomo
creano da millenni
forme, sapori
e profumi fragranti:
il pane
alimentazione
dell'umanità antica
e moderna.

VyTA BOULANGERIE ITALIANA

2. There is maximum design uniformity that slides unobtrusively into the busy station, while allocating ample room for the people waiting to depart, creating a relaxing ambience closely linked to the traditions that are hidden behind the minimalist lines – making Vyta a valid alternative to the world of fast food, and promoting good food culture. The theme of the interior design starts from the traditional image of the bread shop; this is then reduced progressively to its essential features, in the quest for immediate and universal language, that can guarantee the maximum usability in this place of transition.
3-5. The colour scheme corresponds with the ambiance of the railway station and connotates the features of bread. The familiar colours of oak wood harmonise with the pale colours of the flooring and the ceiling, leaving space for monolithic furnishing accessories in black Corian that catalyze the attention through their symbolic purity. There is a large decorative wall consisting of a paste creation symbolising the surface and the fragrance of a bread crust. This element also has strong aesthetic and metaphoric connections and is used as the backdrop to a series of elongated tables and benches. The intelligent use of lighting, enhanced by spherical suspension lamps in chrome-plated metal invites and beckons while amplifying the space.

Floor Plan:
1. Reception
2. Display counter
3. Seating area

Chapter 3: Holistic Design

1. Branding

2. Shopfront Design

3. Interior Design

4. Economical Ways to Update Existing Bakery

Whilst the baked goods purveyor is blessed by the natural attractiveness of the goods he or she sells, it is important to provide a strongly branded purchasing experience in order to stand out from the crowd in an increasingly competitive market. The most effective retail stores are those with a clear sense of identity that is expressed consistently across their logo, signage, graphics, physical store design, product, packaging, customer service, website and marketing. It is becoming more and more important to have a holistic concept and brand strategy in business. Every touch point between the customer and the brand must convey the same messages and style in order to build customer loyalty. Bakery shop owners should research their target markets to identify the profile of the buyers and of the consumers (these are frequently different individuals or groups of people), as well as their local competition and decide upon a strong vision and unique selling proposition. These strategies should then form the basis of the design brief for the store and all visual identity and marketing collateral.

Chapter 3: *Holistic Design*

De Farine & D'eau Fraîche

Designer: Surface3
Location: Montreal, Canada
Project area: 158m²
Project year: 2011
Photographs: Vladimir Antaki

Surface3 was in charge of the brand strategy, the visual identity and the interior design of the pastry boutique. The concept is founded on love, naiveté, and escapism. The first letters of each word of the project name were combined together, forming a unique brand logo, which was extensively used in shopfront and interior elements. In designing the space, Surface3 sought to capture the essence of pastries and the way customers enjoy them in a way that is simple, magical and lasting; from the exchange of pastries as a ritual signifying love and friendship, to the pleasure inherent in simple indulgence. Hanging sculptural lights and custom made furniture finished in dark wood give the feeling that one is in an enchanted forest. The arrangement of space and the many surprising fine details blend with the pastry creations to tell a unique story that is intended to inspire and awaken the youthfulness and magic in everyone.

034

1. Storefront
2. Logos used expansively
3. Display case in white colour to emphasize the product inside
4. The dining table in harmony with floor
5. Display wall
6. Distinctive luminaries dangling above the dining table

035

Floor Plan:
1. Dining area
2. Storage
3. Kitchen
4. Lounge
5. Mechanical room

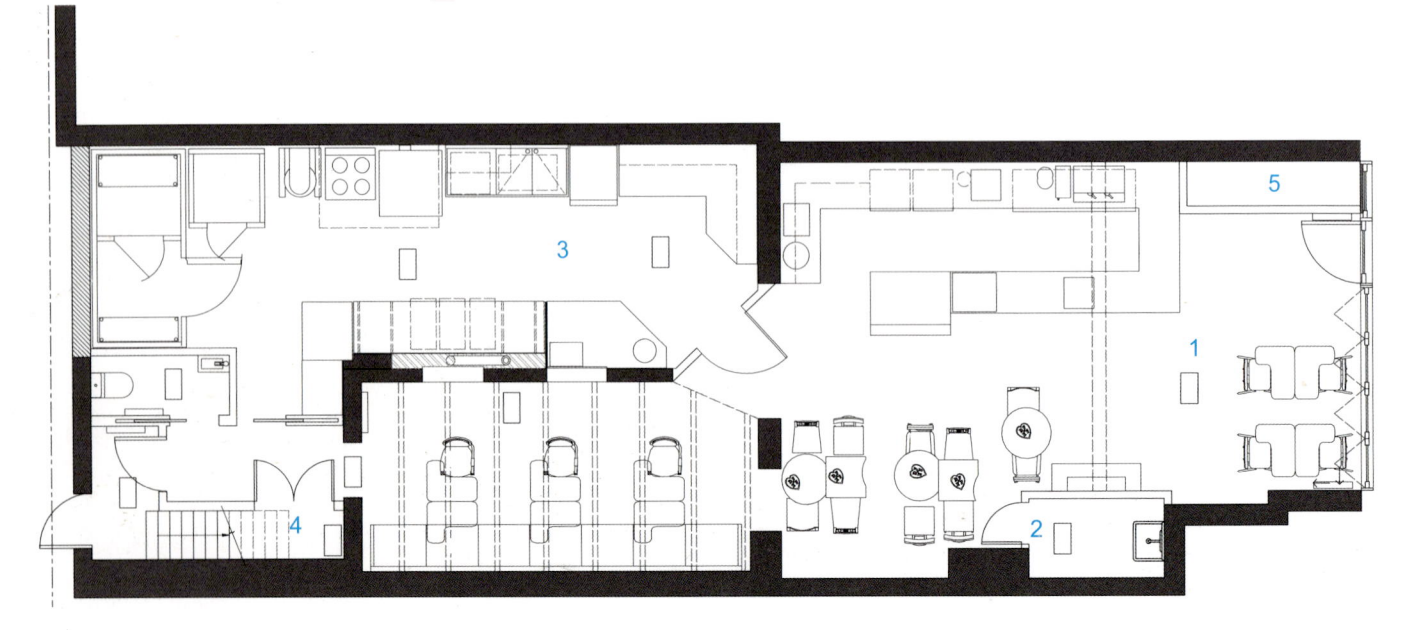

7. Dining tables of various shape
8. The wall of wooden panel contrasting with the leather chair
9. Detail of wooden wall

037

Chapter 3: Holistic Design

↗ MTI notes

1. Branding

The development of strong brand recognition should be an essential part of one bakery's business plan. Creating a brand helps the owner make a statement of what operation is all about. The brand should convey quality, consistency, familiarity, and most importantly, trust. Customers want to come into the bakery and know they will have a good experience because that's what the brand tells them.

Good branding is more than just a catchy slogan or a memorable logo. It's about the entire business and culture. But before one start thinking about writing a catchy slogan that will have millions of people singing your song, you need to take a step back and consider the following questions: where do you see your business in the next five to ten years? Do you plan to franchise your bakery? Who is your target market? Where do you see yourself in the marketplace? How do you differentiate yourself from the competition? What promises do you want to make to your customers about your products?

After answering these questions, the operator will have a better sense of what type of brand he/she wishes to establish for the operation. A strong brand image will bring the company added value, command higher prices and attract better employees. Most of all, it will bring more money. But it needs to be the right brand for the right audience.

Be Specific about the Target Market
Do not try to create a brand that will appeal to everyone. Any operator will end up with a brand that is unclearly defined. Target the brand to the specific demographics to which the bakery will appeal. Consider neighbourhood – is it full of families, students or condo-dwelling urban professionals? Are there a lot of offices? Do you get a good lunch crowd, or after-work crowd? The operator needs to cater the brand image to the right people.

1 Signage
2 Shop Front
3 Promotion
4 Wall
5 Floor
6 Selfie
7 Lighting
8 Tshirt
9 Dress
10 Display
11 witty slogan
12 POS material
13 Story

Create a Positive Perception of the Brand Name

Define the brand using as few words as possible, and deliver the definition to customers. The operator should be able to tell potential customers exactly what to expect from the bakery by stringing together a few key words such as 'homemade', 'comfort', 'stylish', 'elegant', 'fresh' or 'fun'. Just by reading the key words and customers should be able to tell what type of establishment he/she is running.

Brand Consistency

Everything in the bakery must convey what the brand wants to say, including the interior design and décor, menu, prices, food, drinks, uniforms, marketing, advertising, website and customer service. The brand has to be cohesive throughout the entire operation and must reflect its desired image and vision. Developing a powerful brand image involves the entire design of the bakery, from lighting and flooring to powerful graphic images and menu boards. Ensure that the entire look and feel of the bakery is consistent by keeping to a colour scheme. Have a uniform, recognizable style that is apparent throughout the establishment; whether it be inside, outside, online or in print.

Deliver on What the Brand Promises

The most important element of branding is being able to deliver on what the brand is promising. For example, if the operator says that everything he/she sells in the bakery is fresh from oven, make sure that do not outsource any of the products. He/she needs to gain the trust and loyalty of customers by standing by the brand name and what it offers.

POS Materials Help Leave an Imprint of the Brand

Signage and point-of-sale (POS) materials are key in developing instant recognition of the brand. Use POS materials to highlight upcoming specials and promotions, but make sure the brand logo and slogan are prominently featured. It is important to create visually stimulating signs and

Chapter 3: *Holistic Design*

displays so that the customers will remember the images from the POS materials even after they have left the bakery.

Sell Branded Retail Merchandise
Once the operator has established a specific brand, he/she can build on it by offering retail merchandise that features the brand name and slogan, especially if he/she has a particularly witty slogan with a double meaning that can help to launch a successful T-shirt sales operation. Other items to consider include baking equipment, serving dishes, aprons or magnets. The possibilities are endless. Also, not only can the operator stand to make a tidy profit from sales of the merchandise, but it also acts as free advertising for the bakery.

Implementing the above simple steps toward greater brand recognition can make all the difference between everyone knowing the bakery, and being just another name in the phonebook. (Figure 1-5)

Figure 1-5. Branding materials of a bakery shop including bags, brochures, cups, etc..

041

Chapter 3: *Holistic Design*

2. Shopfront Design

With the improvement of living standards, people fond of bakery products are no longer merely satisfied with the taste and they begin to pay more attention to the environment of a bakery. Usually, the first impression of the environment relies more on the shopfront design of a bakery. Many bakery operators failed in the end for lack of an innovative shopfront design.

Zhang Jianhong, a renowned specialist in bakery industry in Taiwan, concluded in one of his books regarding bakery shop design as follows: the innovative design and function of a bakery is not merely to create a space for customers to purchase products, but also to provide solutions to overcome the obstacles and negative conditions that impair business operation; at the same time, it should also be endowed with the ability to stimulate customer's desire to purchase products, which can improve the sales turnover indirectly. Undoubtedly, that is the common target of the operator and designer.

Theme
A certain theme has remarkable effects on the design of a bakery shopfront. A bakery should be given a distinctive style and a certain theme at the beginning.

Symbol
A symbolic meaning which embodies more human factors and is thought provoking can bring unspeakable charm to a bakery. Standing in front of a bakery that can convey a symbolic meaning, the customers may feel have a chance to reflect and communicate.

Unity
Shopfronts of the same brand should be unified in terms of style. At the

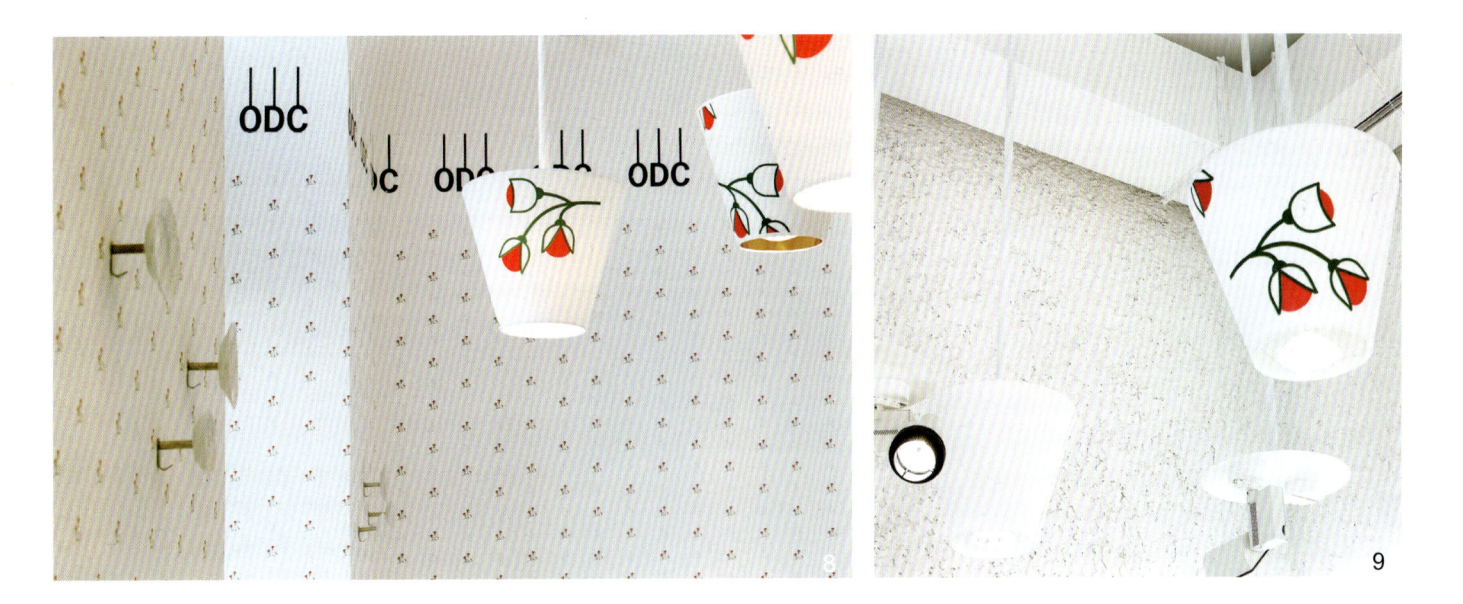

same time, shopfront design should conform with other elements such as product packaging, product display, accessories, media promoting, direct mail advertising, point of purchase and so on.

Diversity
Bakery shopfront design of the same brand can seek subtle changes through a unified style. The designer can break the inertial mode of thinking and make flexible use of the existing elements to create diversified effects. In recent time, shopfront designs are of various styles and innovativeness is of great importance.

Specificity
Specificity plays a rather important role in shop design and forms a contradictory entity with globalization. Specificity has rich connotations and can refer to specific geographic conditions, certain cultural traditions and customs and special features of the building. All of the above can become resources of inspiration for shopfront design, which then can shape the unique cultural feature of architectural form and bring more pleasure to people. (Figure 6-9)

Figure 6-7. Shopfronts of the same brand promoting diversity
Figure 8-9. Shopfront design seeking unity with the interior

Chapter 3: *Holistic Design*

Sprinkles Cupcakes Chicago

Designer: a l m project(Andrea Lenardin Madden, Beth Nelson)
Location: Chicago, USA
Project area: 187.3m²
Project year: 2010
Photographs: Andrea Lenardin Madden

Ever since Oprah announced that Sprinkles' Red Velvet is her favourite cupcake, the Beverly Hills based cupcake-only-bakery began looking for a space in Chicago. They found it on East Walton taking over half of a 2-story former single tenant building.

Sprinkles
3,000 - 8,200 SF
RESTAURANT/RETAIL SPACE
AVAILABLE
AT 54 E. WALTON
SHARON KAHAN
DANNY JACOBSON
CBRE

2

1-4. Sprinkles Cupcakes Chicago is located on East Walton taking over half of a two-storey former single tenant building. The goal of the design was to accentuate the brand's strong vision with an architecture that reflects the product's specificity, purity, and quality. Being presented with the need to create a façade from scratch and recognizing its street presence facing the busy 900 Michigan parking garage, the designers took this opportunity to create a signature façade by introducing brick to tie in with the urban fabric of Chicago and a signature screen system representing a cupcake at architectural scale. The entrance is set back to create a patio – enlivened by Sprinkles' modern colour palette and shaded in the summer, heated in the winter.

5

Floor Plan:
1. Main counter
2. Wall package
3. Kitchen
4. Patio

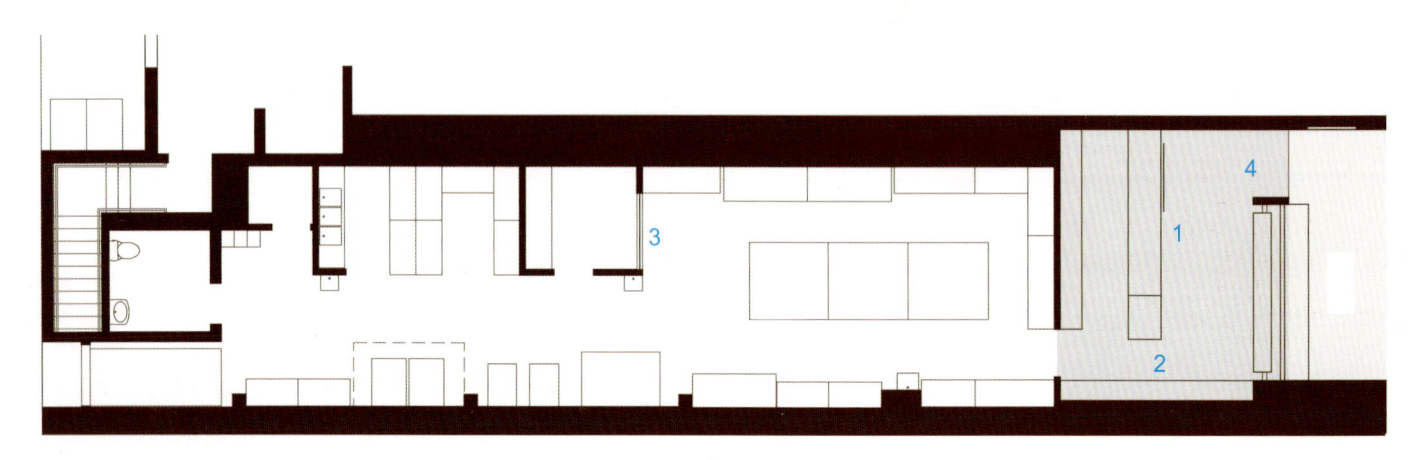

cupcake stand
bench menu
POS Concealed

5-7. The frosted glass door with the clear logo shaped view window allows a peak onto what comes next: upon entering the store one arrives at the heart of every Sprinkles, the Cupcake Array, where 12 daily flavours are meticulously displayed behind a floor to ceiling sheet of glass. The minimalist white oak interior is designed to meld product and architecture in a unified whole – unfolding as an intimate space capable of evoking the memory of European bakeries flooded with the smell of baked goods and awash in natural light.

Chapter 3: Holistic Design

3. Interior Design

The catering space is not presented in a trendy market-favour style and gets rid of the so-called popular design language and form any more, it furthers to consider the humane stories the space tells, providing customers a unique experience in order to achieve its marketing concept.

The designers introduced ideology into human life and express a new thought through the alternation between spatial and functional languages, creating a dialogue between space and life. Through the redefinition of space, the designers and customers can both have a deeper research into the metaphor and concept the commercial activity has brought.

The goal of space design is to provide a fashion statement matching life style. The designers introduced boutique design into the bakery and sell the customers the ordinary product packed in fashion concept. The aesthetics of the space will make the products look much more unique. (Figure 10-13)

Figure 10-13. The continuous pendants emphasize the depth smartly, while the central island station plays a role of partition. The mirror frames and sculpted walls create a mix of elegance for the space. When bread is not simply a product on the shelf, the representative of fashion is not limited in boutique products.

051

Chapter 3: *Holistic Design*

Figure 14. The elongated space poses great challenges for designers and they successfully segregate the space with one side as shop area and the other side as seating area. The kitchen is exists seamless with the shop

Interior Layout

A best practice layout, based upon maximising the functionality of the retail and preparation/manufacture, environment encourages hygienic practices and provides for easier maintenance, improved ergonomics and staff productivity. Kitchens and preparation areas should be based on a flow circle of storage – prep – cook – cool – finish – display – package and sell – wash up. Separate spaces should be allocated for waste, packaging, cold storage, dry storage and staff amenity.

A good front of house layout is characterised by clear sight lines from the shopfront entry to the product display. The shopfront should have high visual impact and strong branding to announce the identity of the business and to attract customers even from a distance. Many bakery retailers enjoy great success from having particularly attractive products displayed in, or near the shopfront.

It is fundamental to ensure adequate queuing space along the front of the baked goods displays, and tiered displays work well to improve product visibility, when customers are lining up along the displays, sometimes several heads deep. If the bakery shop also provides an eat-in offering then tables and chairs should be arranged in such a way as to make the seated customers feel secure and comfortable, whilst not impeding those customers who are purchasing to take away. Bakery shop cafes lend themselves well to creating intimate social spaces in which customers can relax, indulge and catch up with friends and loved ones.

Opportunities for impulse and add on purchases should not be missed and these can be encouraged through having pre-packaged goods displayed on easily accessible shelves where customers can easily grab, pay and go. (Figure 12)

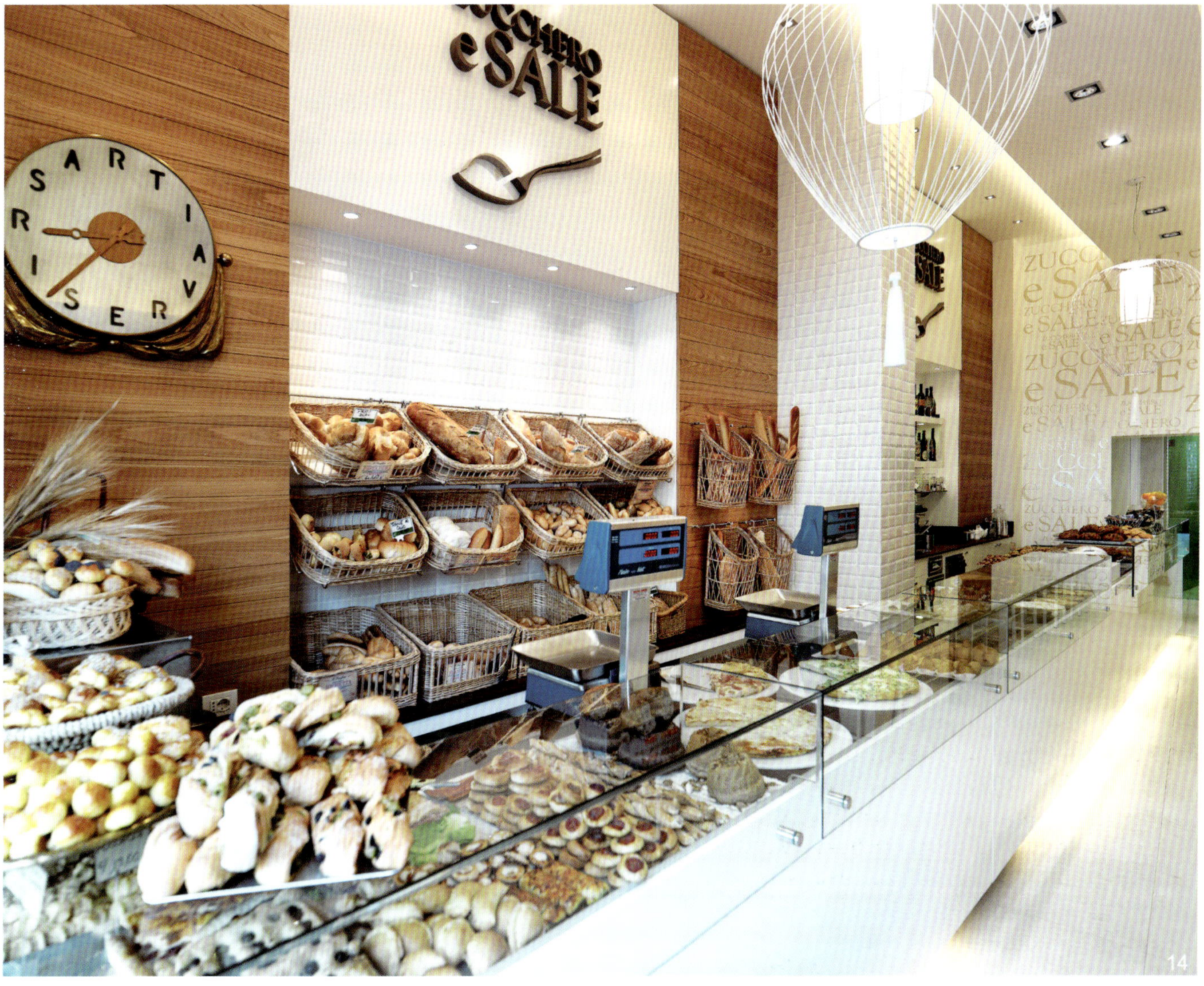

14

Chapter 3: *Holistic Design*

Gourmet Pastry

Designer: 71 Arquitectors
Location: Lisbon, Portugal
Project year: 2011
Photographs: João Morgado

Halfway between the garden of the Principe Real and the Botanical Garden, we can find on the ground floor of an eighteenth century building the most specialized French pastry in the capital, 'Poison d'Amour.'

It was decided that the architecture should assume a role that dictated a discreet dialogue between the sum of light of all colours and the absence of colour (black and white), scenario for a pageant of products that by itself are very colourful, ie, a neutral environment so that the patisserie française can shine.

The pastry develops from a wide entrance hall, divided by an arch. Perpendicular to the façade is the balcony of products on 'Tiger Skin' limestone. In this room customers can admire the exhibition of products, from the petit gateau to the colourful macaroons, served in the tea room on the left.

A belt, disconnected from all the original structure has been connected, and all the elements, walls, ceilings and floors were painted matte black, leaving only the sight of the stone cladding of limestone of the arc that is presented in the lobby. The immaculate white belt surrounds all spaces, creating a relation between the various compartments, and at the same time allows to support any kind of decorative intervention by the customer. The belt allowed to pass most of the infrastructures from behind, relying on the support structure of the belt, and avoid the opening of rocky debris, thereby making the work faster and economical. All existing joinery were replaced by more slender steel profiles and without beams, allowing to establish a stronger link between the interior and the exterior.

In the garden path customers pass by the left side of the sanitary facilities, following the cafeteria and the respective counter also in 'Tiger Skin'. From the cafeteria they can see the garden/terrace which stretches itself over the botanical garden. The cafeteria area also accesses the laboratory/kitchen, the sanitary facilities for staff and the storage area.

NAKED HANGING LIGHTS

1. Outdoor dining area – the white colour applied to seek harmony with the interior
2. The colours of white (wall) and black (ceiling) forming a perfect background for colourful products
3. The display case set adjacent to the entrance
4. The chandeliers and the wall painting evoking senses of European style

055

Black & White theme

Floor Plan:
1. Laboratory
2. Cafeteria
3. Storage
4. Exhibition hall

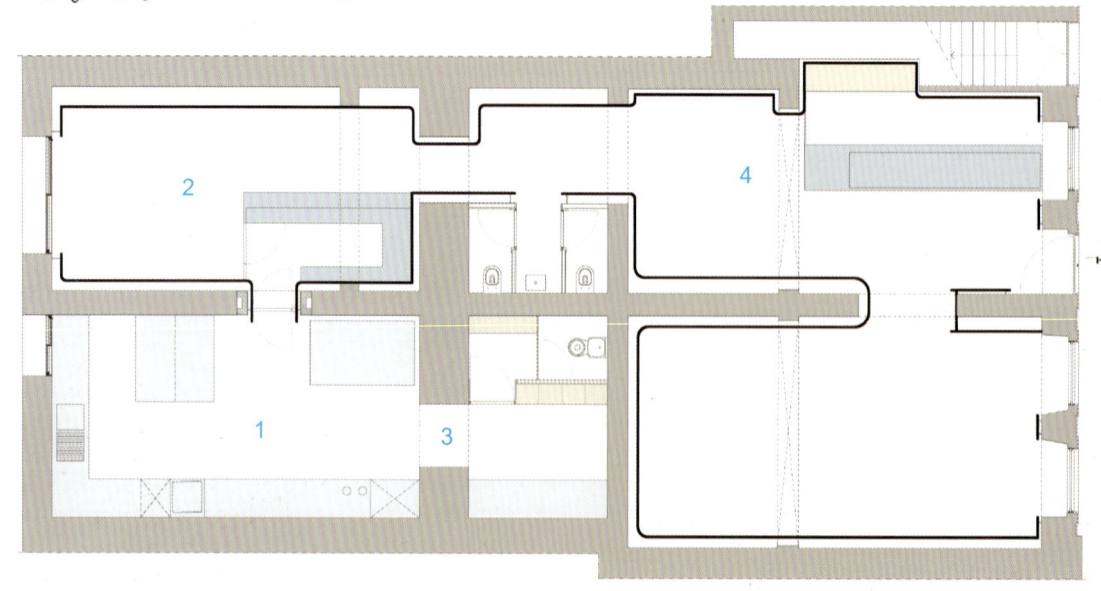

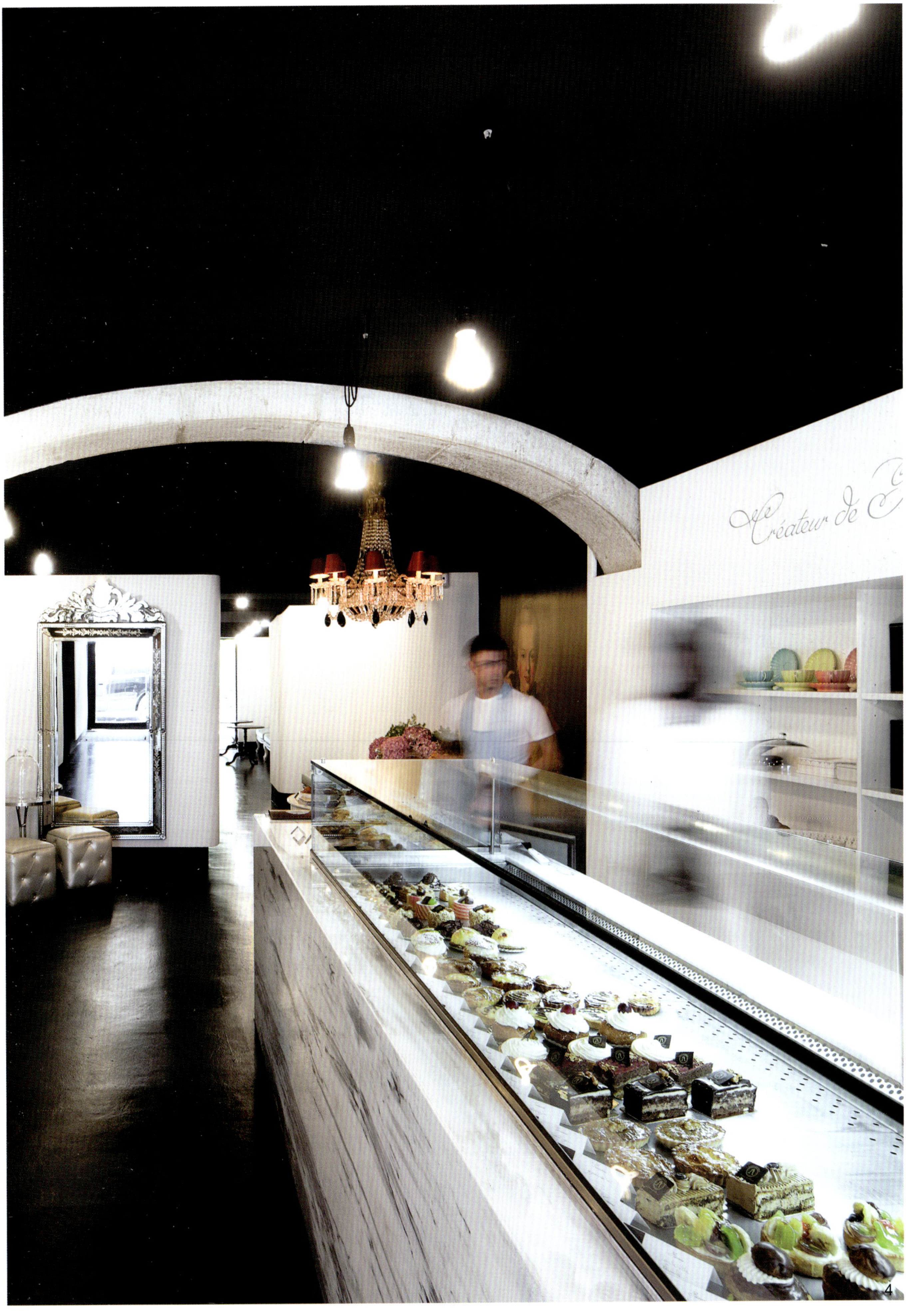

4

5. The cafe bar at the back of the space
6-8. Dining area separated from other space

059

Chapter 3: *Holistic Design*

Treiber Bakery & Café I

Designer: RAISERLOPES Architekten
Location: Stuttgart, Germany
Project area: 115m²
Project year: 2011
Photographs: RAISERLOPES Architekten

The new bakery is located outside Stuttgart. The main intention was to integrate urban and rustic traditional elements in the design. A variety of zones for different length of stay and the potential for communication are needed. Therefore they have planned a standing area, a open seating area with armchairs, a long bench and a small semi-closed seating area, for people looking for some privacy to read a book or work with a laptop.

A wooden platform divides the space and enlarges it optically. The red felt-covered bench joins the different height of floor and platform, but also plays with it, since there are two different seating heights. Young persons or children standing on the platform have an equal footing. The podium is located towards the window, furnished with small coloured tables and chairs, like a living room. A blade ceiling in brushed larch defines the space under which guests can make themselves comfortable in 'Hartz IV' chairs.

A room-in-room-solution – completely lined with felt and therefore sound-absorbing – allows peaceful talking, sitting, reading or working. The variety of lamps emphasize the independent character of the small and cozy space.

blade ceiling
variety of lamps
coat hanger
urban style
Rustic Floor

Floor Plan:
1. Display counter
2. Semi-closed seating area
3. Open seating area
4. Standing area

coloured table & chairs

061

1-3. The display counter set parallel with semi-closed seating area
4. Open seating area opposite the display counter featuring distinctive ceiling and colourful tables and chairs

062

Sketch

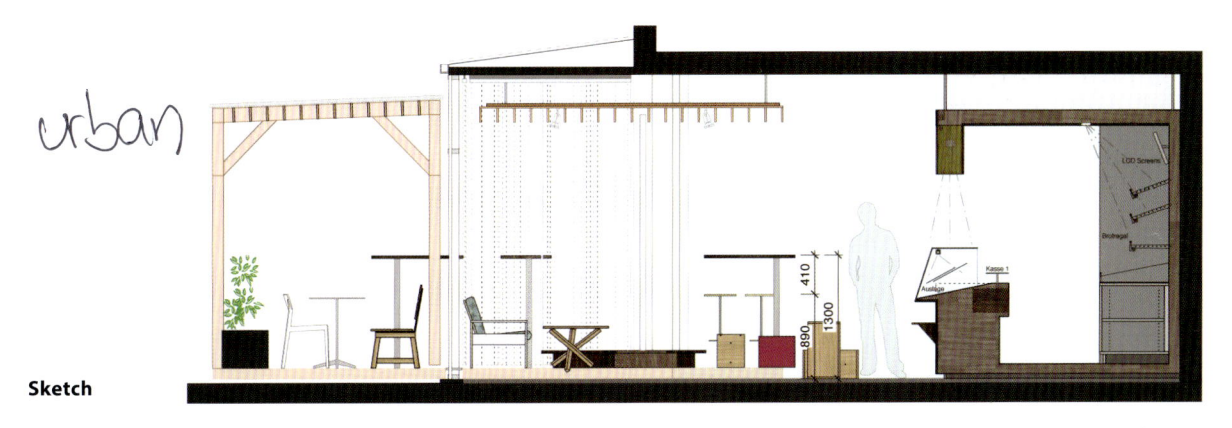

varis lighting

colored chair

Section

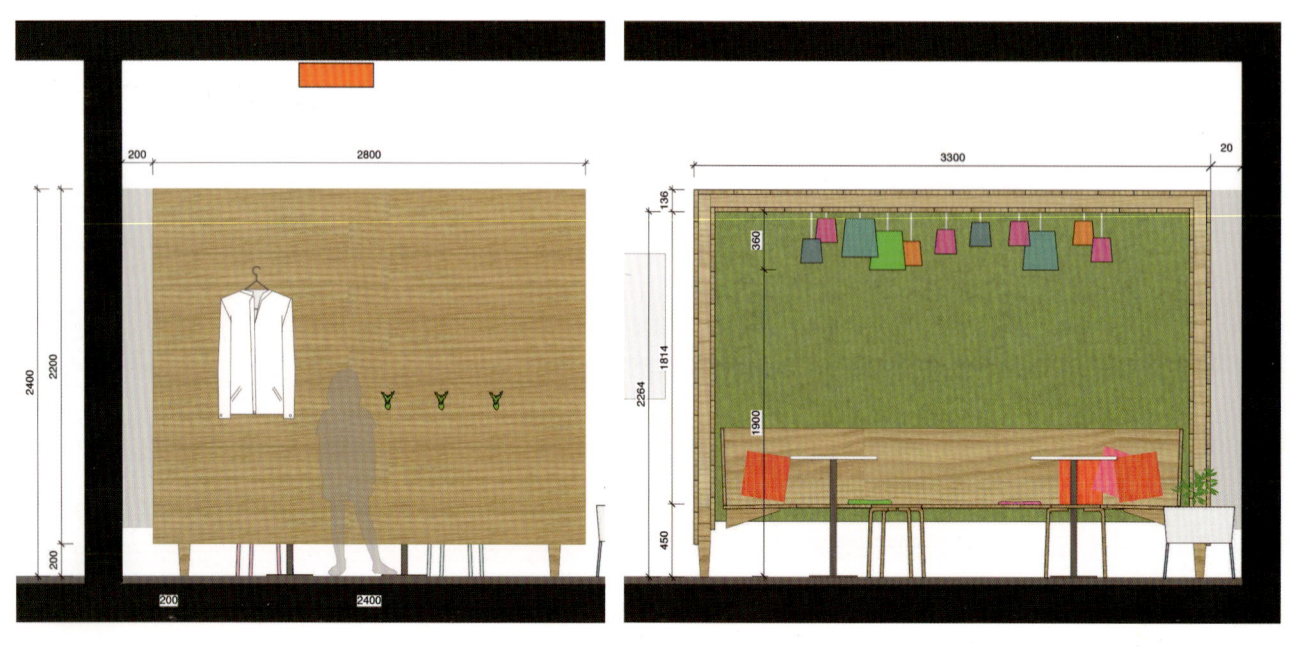

064

5-6. Semi-closed seating area interior : clusters of lamps and fabric cushions creating a homely atmosphere

Chapter 3: Holistic Design

Treiber Bakery & Café II

Designer: RAISERLOPES Architekten
Location: Sielmingen, Germany
Project area: 115m²
Project year: 2011
Photographs: RAISERLOPES Architekten

The new branch of the bakery is located next to the city hall in the centre of Sielmingen, near Stuttgart. The design fuses traditional skills like coziness and quality with contemporary language of forms and materials. A well arranged floor plan with different zones of seating areas is furnished with new design and old findings.

A white Corian counter with freshly baked goods welcomes the customers. They can either purchase bakery good or have a short coffee break at the standing area. The counter-area is framed by a backwall of limed oak and a black ceiling with a surface directed lighting as well as accent illumination. The standing area is furnished with dark stained oak tables and black bar stools.

The seating area is situated in a 65-square-metre room next door. The wall in between was opened and a continuous floor covering (grey mosa tiles) connects the two spaces. The "living room" adopts the limed oak back wall illuminated from the cut-out ceiling. The integrated door to the bathrooms achieve a holistic surface and a calm ambiance. The other wall is covered with wallpaper and shows framed pictures of the history of the bakery.

The bench of dark-brown leather with dark tables seams and defines the room, but also allows the flexibility to put tables and chairs together. A big oak table invites bigger groups for a stay. Chairs from the fleamarket were coated in different colours. These furniture, a table with bamboo chairs and a chest of drawers give the interior a distinctive visual character. Built-in spots and a chandelier, also from the flea market, in the centered round ceiling-cutout ensure good illumination.

Handwritten annotations on photo:
- content & bread displ.
- beverage storage
- framed menu
- beverage stora
- POS
- multiple POS x3
- clear label
- vanity danish
- convection oven to Reheat
- meal offer
- coffee menu

1. Eye-catching decorative features dangling from the ceiling adding interest to the dining area
2. Display counter with fresh baked foods

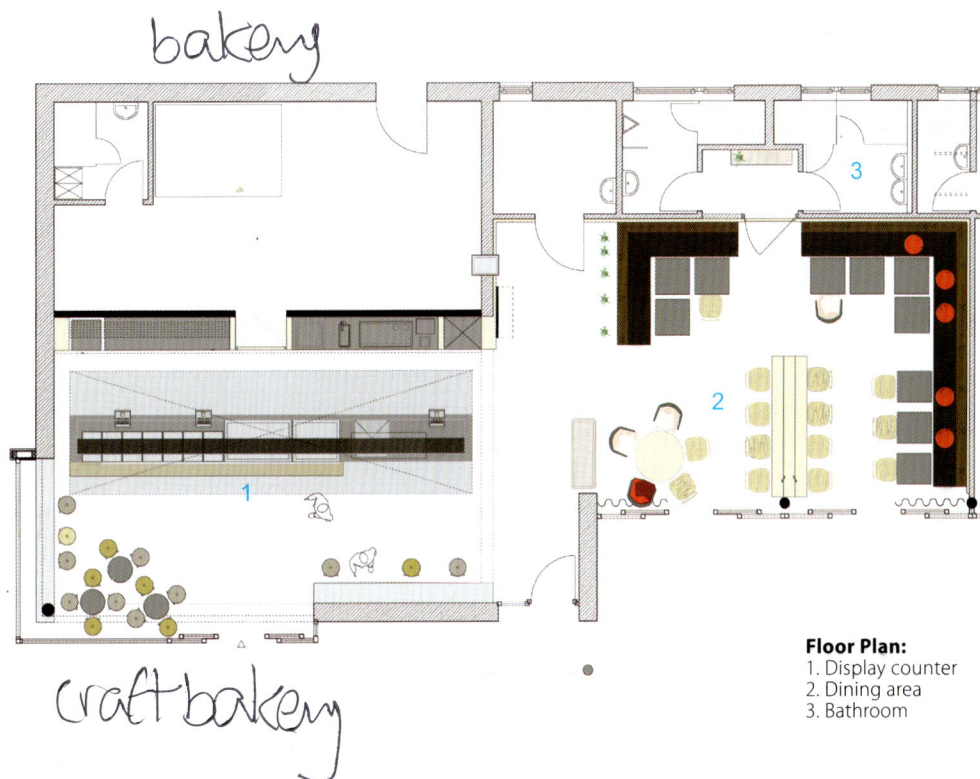

Handwritten on floor plan: bakery / craft bakery

Floor Plan:
1. Display counter
2. Dining area
3. Bathroom

067

Limed oak   black ceiling

cutout ceiling

contempory style   wall paper   vanity colourful chairs   history of Bakery (old picture)

3. Display counter, standing area and seating area emphasizing different styles
4-5. Seating area featuring colourful tables and chairs

069

Chapter 3: *Holistic Design*

TOMASELLI

Designer: Studio Giuseppe Dondoni SGD
Location: Milan, Italy
Project area: 250m²
Project year: 2011
Collaboration: CRS

This project is a collaboration between SGD and CRS, and where designers combine different values to define new spaces but with traditional content. After a study of the functional areas of service and work comes the expressive gesture that summarises all the shapes and signs design.

This highly expressive space brings out the post to be on display and even tweak with the idea of crossing lines with the stained glass project, as if there were no boundaries. The great curve that marks out eyes from the ceiling frames the essence of the space, the gesture of which draws in front view a giant T as Tomaselli and the barrier of the loft. Behind it continues laboratories and kitchen, and finally extends to the outdoor area.

Clear colours and hints of the Nordic design highlight each other. The lime green walls of the loft create a visual separation from the big wooden T. Items made of natural materials such as baskets containing bread tied on the walls with ropes, curtains in scenic canvas and especially willow structure holding cash register create a new effect, welcoming and dynamic.

Lighting changes according to different time in a day and different environments, creating a multipurpose space from breakfast to lunch to afternoon snack.

2

Lime green wall paint
3
giant T. company name
Storage
bread basket
tiled wall
Rustic tile

1. Shopfront: large expanse of glass completely showing the interior scene
2. Back door leading to the outdoor dining
3. Display counter adjacent to the entrance
4. The giant 'T' behind display counter symbolising the name of the shop
5. The willow basket holding cashier
6. Loft: upstair dining
7. General view of loft and ground floor area
8. Stairs leading to loft
9. The lime green walls of the loft creating a peaceful atmosphere

Elevation

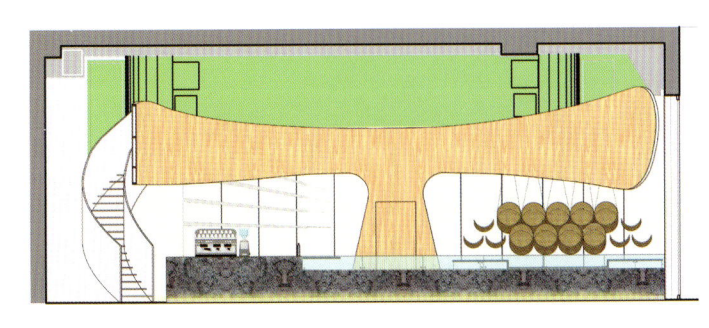

Floor Plan:
1. Counter
2. Dining area
3. Bathroom

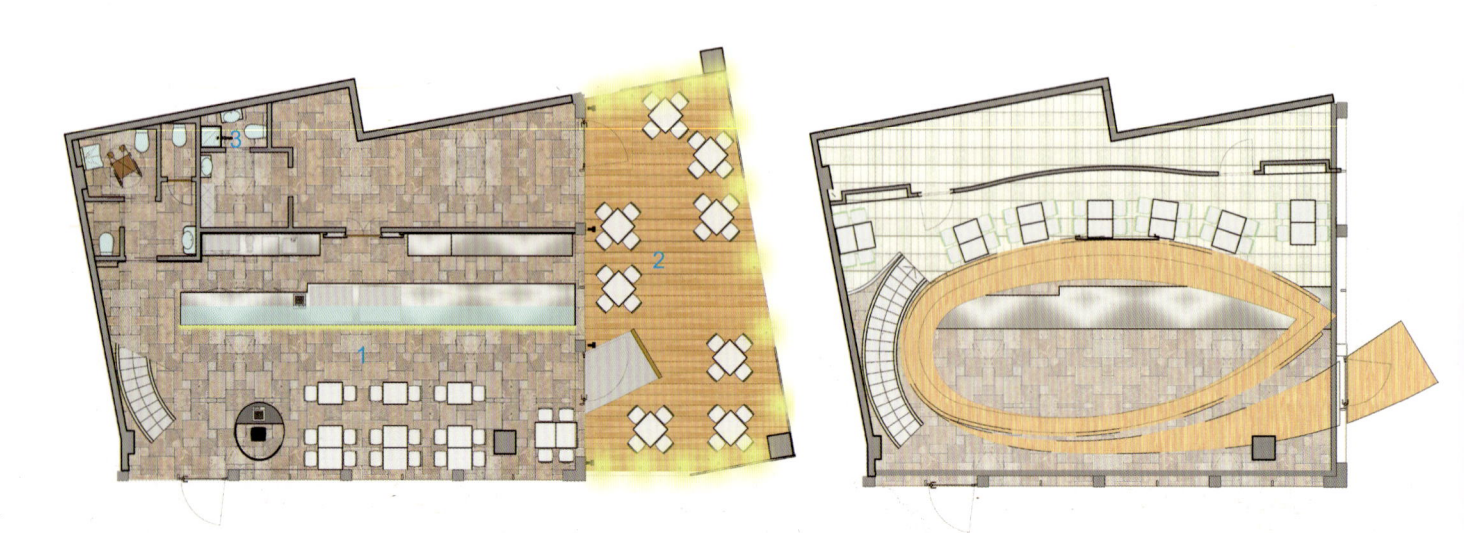

075

Chapter 3: *Holistic Design*

The Mill's Workshop

Designer: Sandra Tarruella Interioristas
Location: Manuel de Falla, Spain
Project area: 260m²
Project year: 2010
Photographs: Jordi Sarrà

The project consisted on opening the workshop to the shop, and the shop to the street. By establishing a visual connection between all spaces, customers could realise and understand the entire manufacturing process and all the steps it entailed, the ingredients and the traditional process that had been gradually hidden away in the back of the shop. The exhibition of different types of bread serves as the backdrop that unites the manufacturing and selling areas. This screen, made out of several turning wicker baskets supported by an iron structure, is the leading feature of the whole space and the link between the two areas.

The jointless cement counter, which is a visual extension of the floor, is a hefty element that serves as support for a topography of blocks of different woods and sizes, where breads are displayed. The suspended ceiling is finished in whitened cloth and there is a play with different heights, inspired by the linen used for leavening bread dough. The iron panelled frames, functional wooden furniture and bar counter finished in white marble complete the list of materials that dress up the space and create an atmosphere that is sober, refined, and industrially casual.

industrially casual

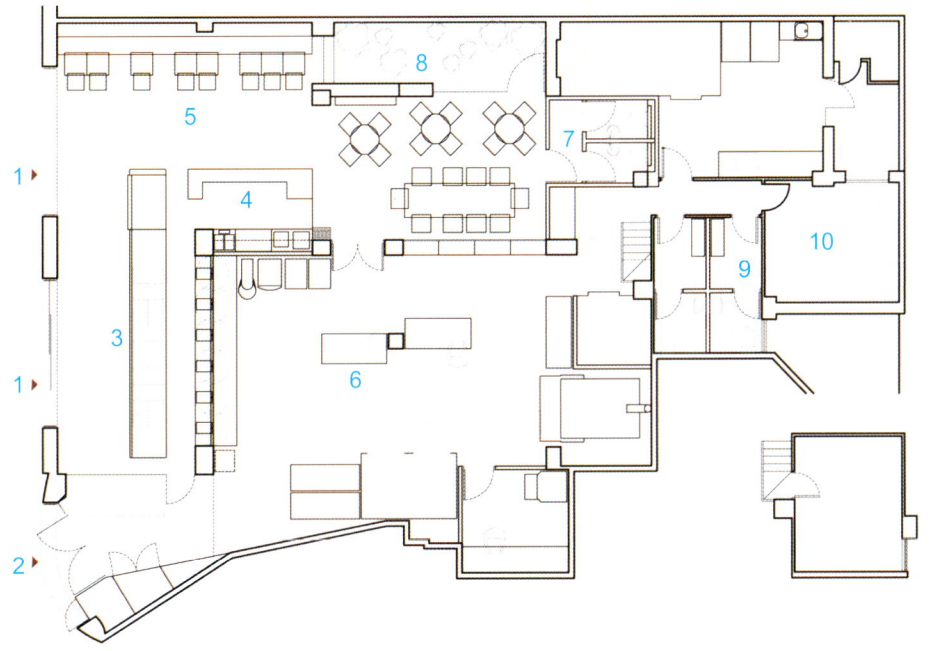

Floor Plan:
1. Principal access
2. Merchandise access
3. Bread shops
4. Bar cafeteria
5. Tasting area
6. Workshop
7. Bathroom
8. Patio
9. Cloakrooms
10. Storage/Installation

077

industrilly causal →

basket. iron, frame →

vainty wooden block Jointless as tray cement counter

BAGUETTE DE L'OBRADOR. 200G - 1,10€
BARRA DE QUART. 200G - 1,00€
PA DE PAGÈS. 800G - 2.50€
PA DE VIENA. 200G - 1,20€
PA DE PAGÈS. 400G - 1,60€
CIABATTA. 200G - 1.40€

1. Diversified fresh products on the counter
2. Shopfront along the street - large expanse of glass bringing inside views out
3. The display counter separated from the workshop by a display wall
4. Bar cafeteria emphasizing simple style
5. Tasting area behind workshop
6. Workshop

visual
ingredient
storage
display

functional
wooden
furniture

Chapter 3: *Holistic Design*

Doclimanie Bar & Pastry Shop

Designer: Studiounodesign Nuti & Bartolomeo
Location: Pisa, Italy
Project area: 60m²
Project year: 2010
Photographs: Simone H. Rocchi

Embracing interior design styling of decor object and furniture's complements, the design concept is always trying to achieve a balance between function and beauty. The target is the valorisation of the spaces and forms to reach the harmony of an ambient by using advanced technical resources that permits to reach amazing achievement. Earnest and professional details attention in every step of projection and freshness of the ideas and proposals are the features of this project.

A new and even more effective framework is created in the recent restyling of the Doclimanie Bar & Pastry Shop. Here the classic decor is pushed towards a contemporary influence, putting the artistic value first and a natural beauty by means of precise variations of tonality.

The concept follows the traditional functionality of the pastry shop, keeping the big display windows at the entrance. The borderline of the bar counter has been made out of a giant frame in Korian white and a façade in leather button cushioning. This linearity continues on to the service table positioned in a small-size room.

The small room is completely covered with vertically striped wallpaper around a leather sofa. The enormous mirrors, made by a genuine Tuscan artisan, are outlined with decorative shapes amplified by an LED backlight. The deco art style lamps confirm the preference of a retro atmosphere.

Classic contemporary design

contemporary

Leather cushions design

classic

classic Contemporain design
leather button
large display

Floor Plan:
1. Display area
2. Bathroom
3. Changing room
4. Storage

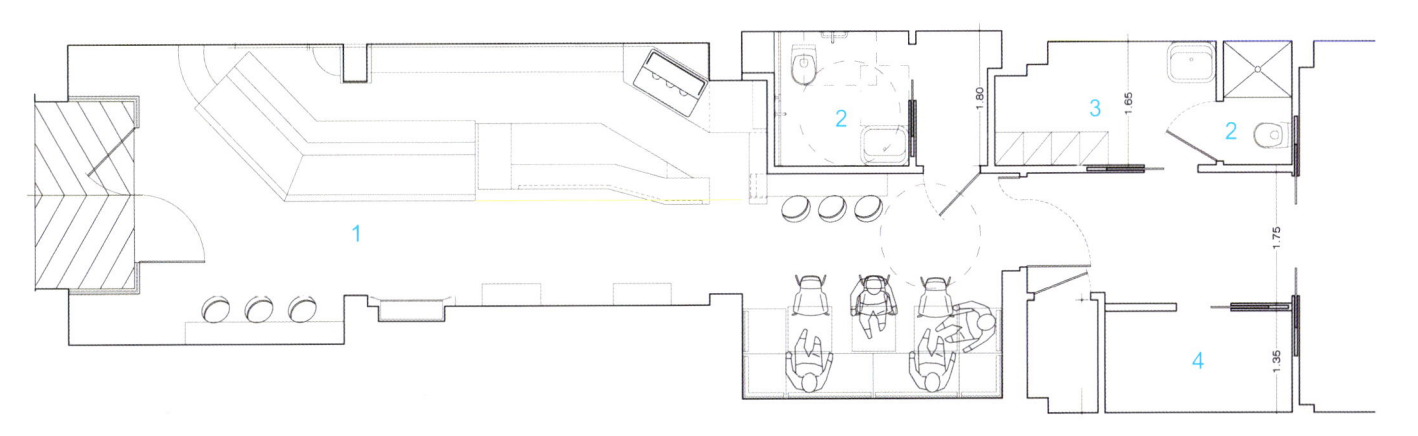

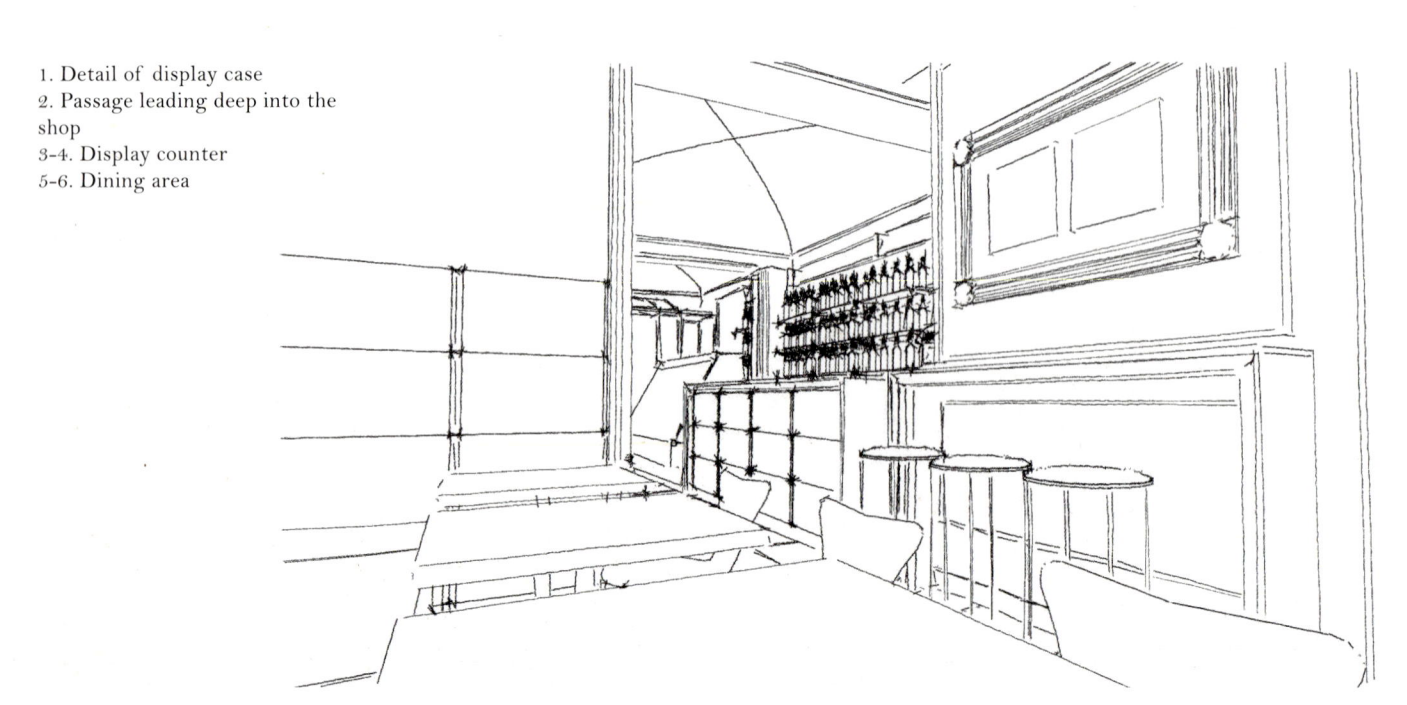

1. Detail of display case
2. Passage leading deep into the shop
3-4. Display counter
5-6. Dining area

6

Chapter 3: *Holistic Design*

Zucchero & Sale

Designer: Andrea Langhi Design
Location: Milan, Italy
Project area: 100m²
Project year: 2010
Photographs: Daniele Domenicali

This venue aims to modernise the traditional bakery using natural materials such as raw wood, glazed ceramic coatings and the tables for exposition, but composing them in a more modern way according to a linear design.

The elongated shape of the room proposed to conceive the shop as a journey to the discovery of flavours and specialties – starting from the front door and crossing a long corridor along the counter - a long glass counter displays all the baked goods prepared in the laboratory visible at the bottom of the venue. The backstage is made by natural wood and it frames some vertical columns covered with diamond ceramic tiles, like those used in 1950s, which are the only colour point in the whole white place. Some wall mirrors visually expand the space. On the top, the embossed inscriptions, report the logo of the shop. On the other side, high shelves with stools have been provided, due to the little width of the room.

In a bright environment, white is the predominant colour. From bread to cakes, from pastry to the coffee shop area, all products are clearly visible and are the real attraction of the place, attracting the attention of customers and stimulating sales. The choice of white just serves to enhance the products, creating an ideal stage for the sale. The lamps (designed by Karman) give a creative touch to the environment, as well as the decorated wall at the bottom of the room.

ZUCCHERO e SALE

1. The European style shopfront
2. Detail of display wall
3. Display counter extending from entrance
4. Standing area
5-6. Door leading into the laboratory

Handwritten annotations:
- ceremi
- single deck display
- raw wood
- white base color
- ceremic
- designer lamps
- bread # cake # pastry # coffee all visible

CAFFE PANE

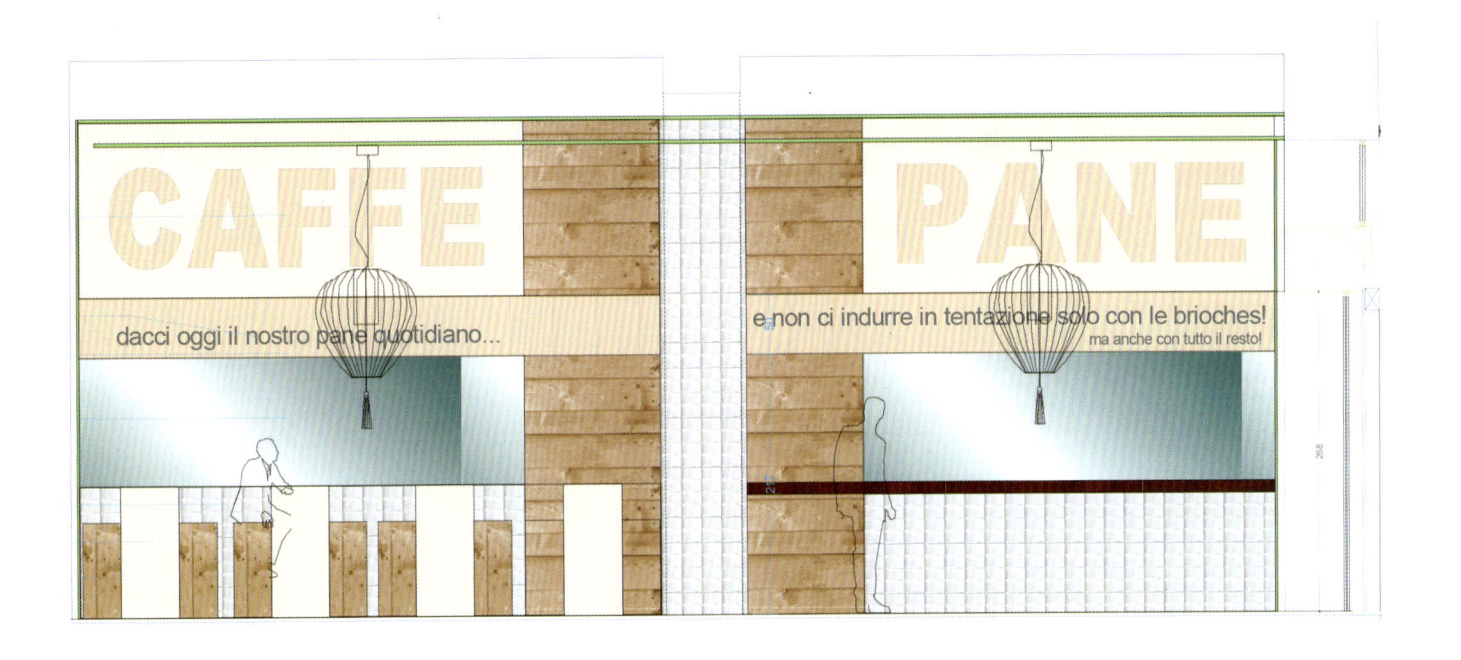

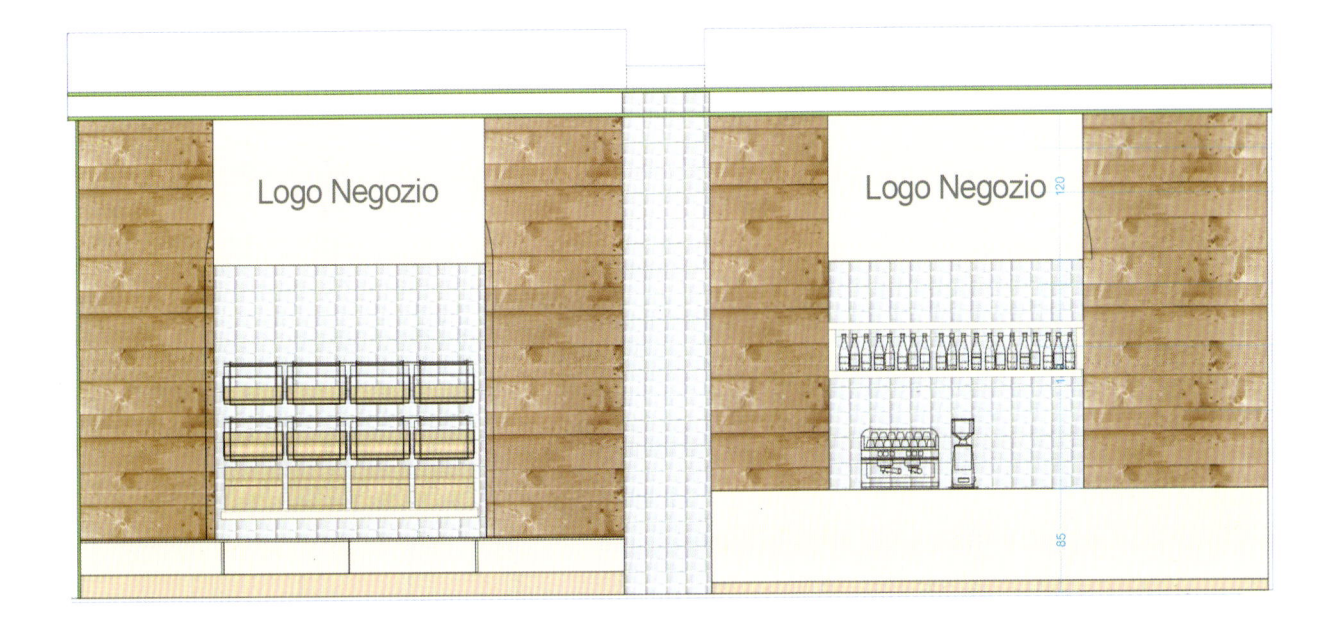

dacci oggi il nostro pane quotidiano... e non ci indurre in tentazione solo con le brioches!
ma anche con tutto il resto!

Logo Negozio   Logo Negozio

Sections

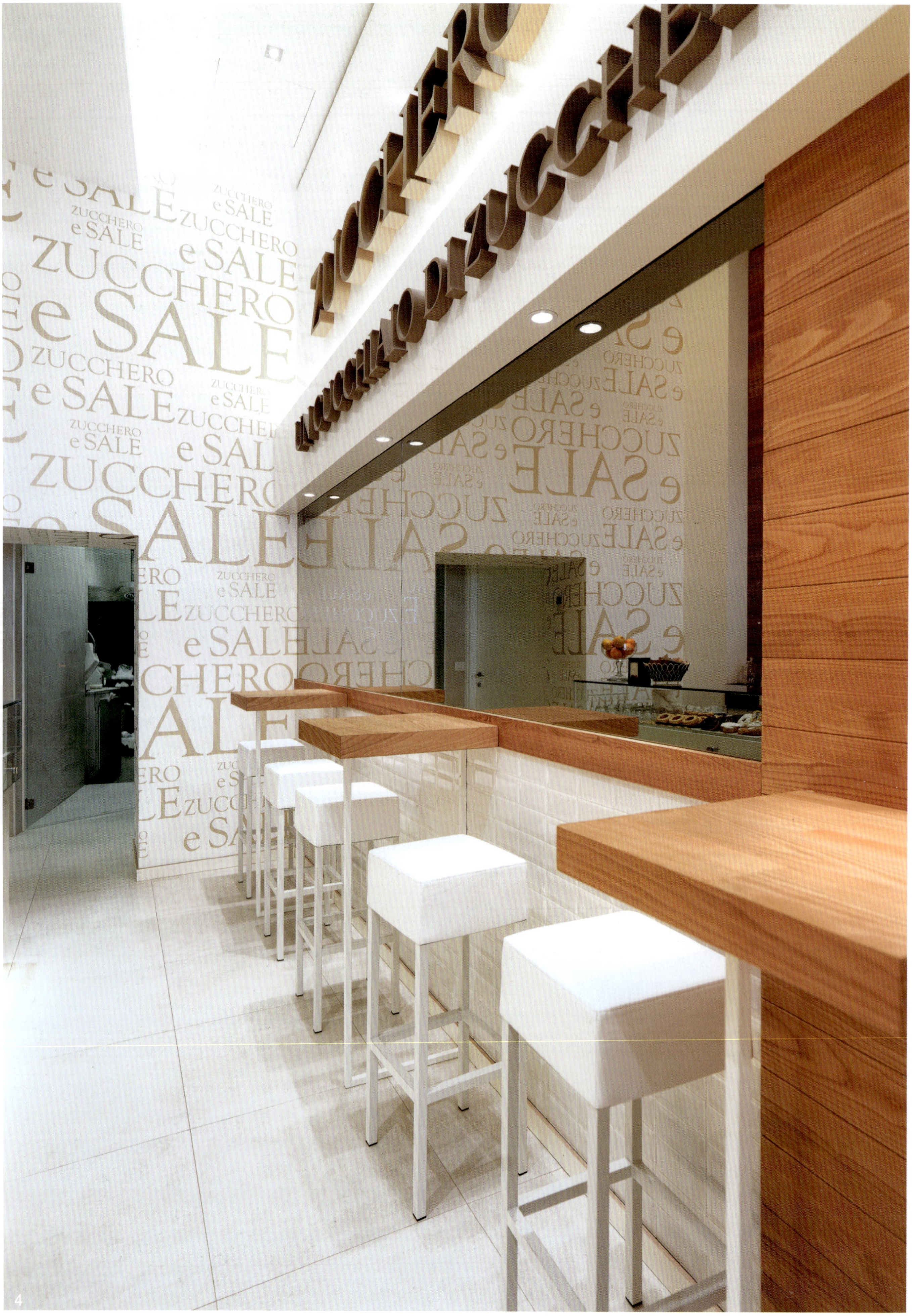

4

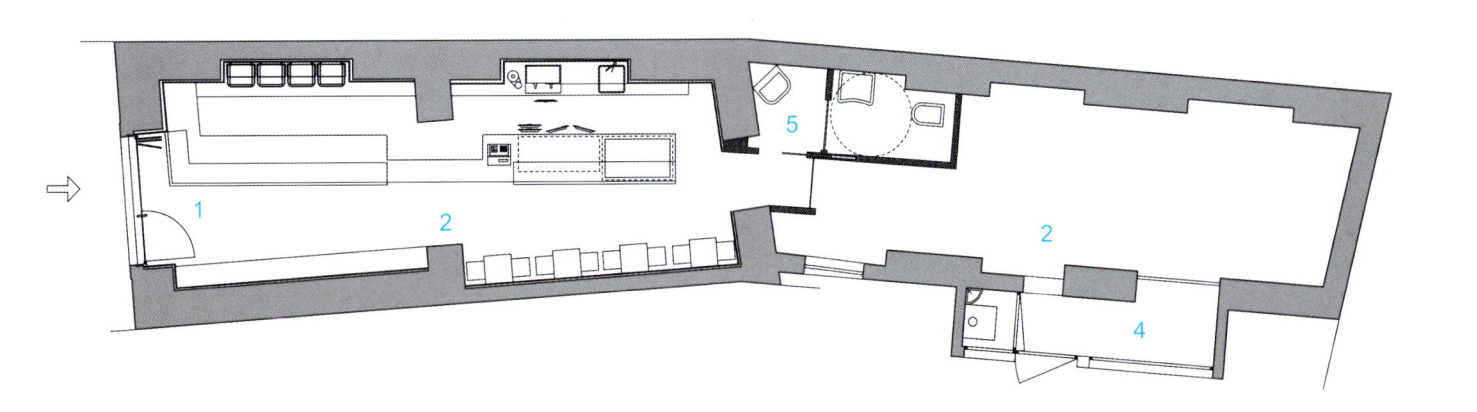

Floor Plan:
1. Entrance
2. Shop area
3. Laboratory
4. Staff restroom
5. Public bathroom

093

Chapter 3: *Holistic Design*

Wood-fired Oven Bakery in Vienna

Designer: Architekt Jürgen Radatz
Location: Vienna, Austria
Project area: 105m²
Project year: 2010
Photographs: Erich Hussmann/image industry

The conversion of an old antiquarian shop into a wood-fired oven bakery occupies the ground floor of a protected building in Spiegelgasse, in the central district of Vienna. On the main street elevation following the removal of the superimposed wooden shopfront, the original rendered façade of the building was restored. The insertion of new openings reproduced the partition and proportions of the existing historical windows on the floors above. In particular the bakery entrance door was located under a prominent existing semi-circular window with original wrought iron work. On the adjoining party-wall street elevation the conservation requirements were more relaxed thus a new wide glass window could be installed. The central lower part of the glazing can be opened from the inside through a sliding window to allow food and drink sales directly into the street in keeping with the city tradition.

Off the central courtyard of the building the old horse stables were converted into an area for the preparation and baking of goods. The space is linked to the bakery shop through the building and houses the bakery equipment with the exception of the main oven. The wood-fired oven, especially designed and made for this project, is the central element between the shop and the preparation area and can be glanced by customers over the baked goods counter. Bakery clients can enjoy a range of freshly made baked products, sandwiches and soups at the bar along the wall opposite the counter. The bar is also provided with high stools for comfort and a street view through the wide glass window.

The choice of surface materials mirrors the organic and highest quality of the bakery food production: oil finished oak wood for the furniture and stainless steel for the counters, natural stone for the floors and tiles and plaster finishes for the walls. The wood-fired oven is brick-clad with untreated steel doors. The bakery area is flooded with indirect light bouncing down from the white ceiling.

white ceiling
reflecting lights

For Children

wood burning oven is center to

1. Shopfront view along the street
2. Shop area : street scenes being brought in through the giant glass window
3-4. The lower part of the glazing is used to sell products to customers on the street without coming in and the distinctive display case
5. Preparation area : white as the main colour to emphasize cleanness
6. Staff working in front of the wood-fried oven
7. Wooden display case

Floor Plan:
1. Principal access
2. Merchandise access
3. Bread shops
4. Bar cafeteria
5. Tasting area
6. Workshop

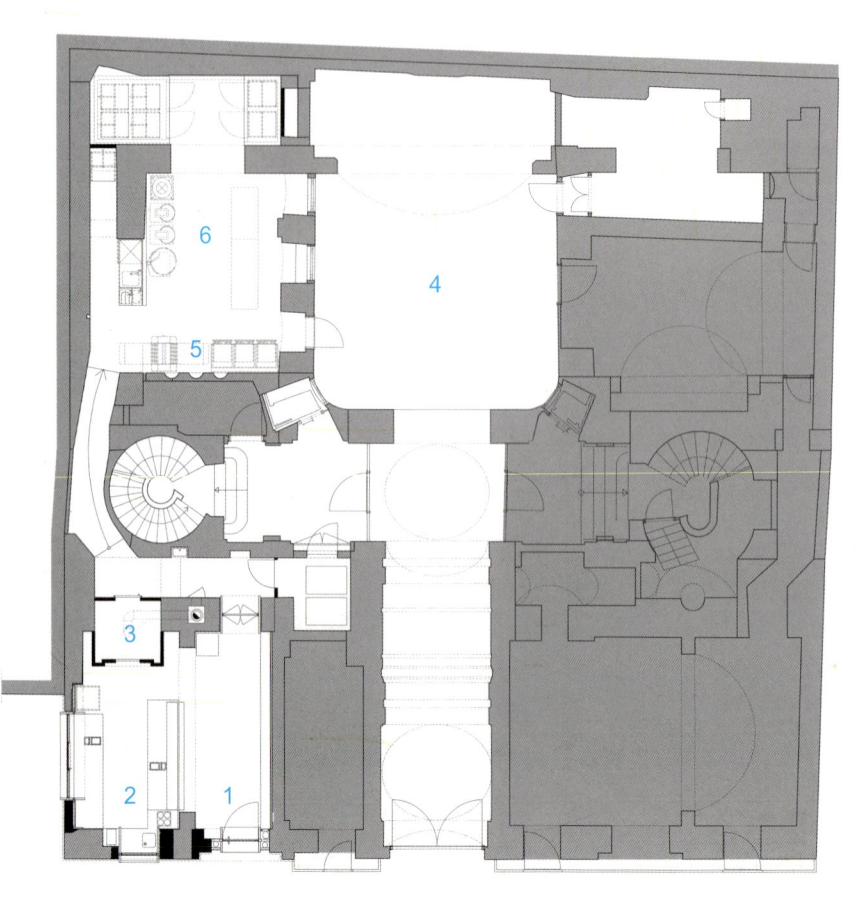

098

7

Chapter 3: Holistic Design

[Handwritten margin notes:]
keywords — graphic + colour, material: warm colors, luxury, indulgence, celebrat[ion], beiges, off white, less colourful graphic, colourful logos, natural material, mid tone wood, natural stone, cane baskets, farmhouse, flour sacks, reclaimed bricks, exposed pipework, wood crates, blackboard, retro signs

Colour & Graphic Design

Most often, baked goods are associated with warm colour tones. It is likely the sense of luxury, indulgence and celebration that sees bakery shops decked out in reds and golds. In European countries there is a tradition of black, or warm dark timbers, with white and gold decoration in bakery shop design. More recently we've occasionally seen the introduction of playful oranges and yellows added to the pallet of bakery shop fit-outs in Asia.

Bakery shop colours are commonly drawn from the ingredients such as wheat, balanced with beiges and off whites associated with flour.

Graphic design is generally not dominant in bakery stores because the product itself is so visually enticing. Rather, environmental graphics are largely restrained to supporting patterns or logo/visual identity elements. Traditionally the fonts used for bakery shop signage have been highly decorative and calligraphic in style, but more recently we see refined serif typefaces used for an air of restrained style and elegance, or playful sans serif typefaces used to attract younger customers to lower price point offerings.

[Handwritten margin note: Less graphics to allow product to stand out, colourful logo used]

Materials

Bakery shops are often fitted out with reference to natural materials evoking a rustic, farm house aesthetic. This is characterised by the use of light to mid-toned timbers, light natural stone, cane baskets and off white paint colours.

The current general trend, in retail, towards industrial and warehouse styled interiors sees the introduction of 'found materials' such as hessian flour sacks, reclaimed bricks and timbers, exposed pipe work and services, wooden crates, black board menus and retro signage. This style has found its way into cake and bakery shops in what seems to be contemporary design's search for a sense of authenticity and reminiscence.

Many bakery stores seek to express elegance and indulgence through the use of warm, dark timbers, black marble and fine gold detailing. This is usually supported by European styled bent wood furniture, decorative detailing to table bases, statement pendant lighting, ornate supporting patterns and highly professional signage.

Whatever the look that a cake or bakery shop is aiming to achieve, the overriding factor in selecting materials and finishes is that they must be durable to high traffic and must be easy to clean. (Figure 15)

Chapter 3: *Holistic Design*

Rossi & Rossi

Euro design

Designer: Andrea Langhi
Location: Milan, Italy
Project area: 73m²
Project year: 2010
Photographs: Andrea Langhi

Many people might think customers will visit a bakery simply because of the quality of its goods, but the interior design and space of a bakery are equally important in attracting new and old customers and adding to the overall shopping experience. Calacatta white marble, mahogany wood, polished steel, mirrors, glass and shiny brass! But surely this is a bakery.

Located in Milan Italy, Rossi & Rossi bakery was designed using modern concept with soft colour complete with amazing lighting. The bakery atmosphere fell so comfortable, elegant and emitted a unique sense of place that provides a whole range of sensory impressions. The designers create bright lighting in the bar area and contrasting with brighter lighting in the lower galley area. They also provide a flexible lighting system to encourage art on the walls. Eye-catching elements are added in several locations within the bakery.

Making a first impression is crucial in business, and the only way to make a good first impression with a store is not through the food, but what the customers see as soon as they walk through the door. In order to bring guest vision together, Andrea Langhi uses a story/colour board to attach guest tear sheets, finishes, fabric swatches, photos, design sketches, clippings and paint chips. This will be a roadmap for making decisions about what to buy and use. Paint three-inch by three-inch wood panels with colours and work around space from dark spots to nearby windows to see how colours work in different situations.

Basket

Calcatta White Blanco

Baked Product Std wt lit display

1. Shopfront view: the colourful interior world being showed completely through the giant glass door
2. Calacatta white marble display counter and floor and mahogany wall creating a perfect background for the baked products
3. Light spreading from ceiling and being reflected by smooth surface to add brightness and playfulness
4. The white stools and tables along the staircase creating a simple dining area

4

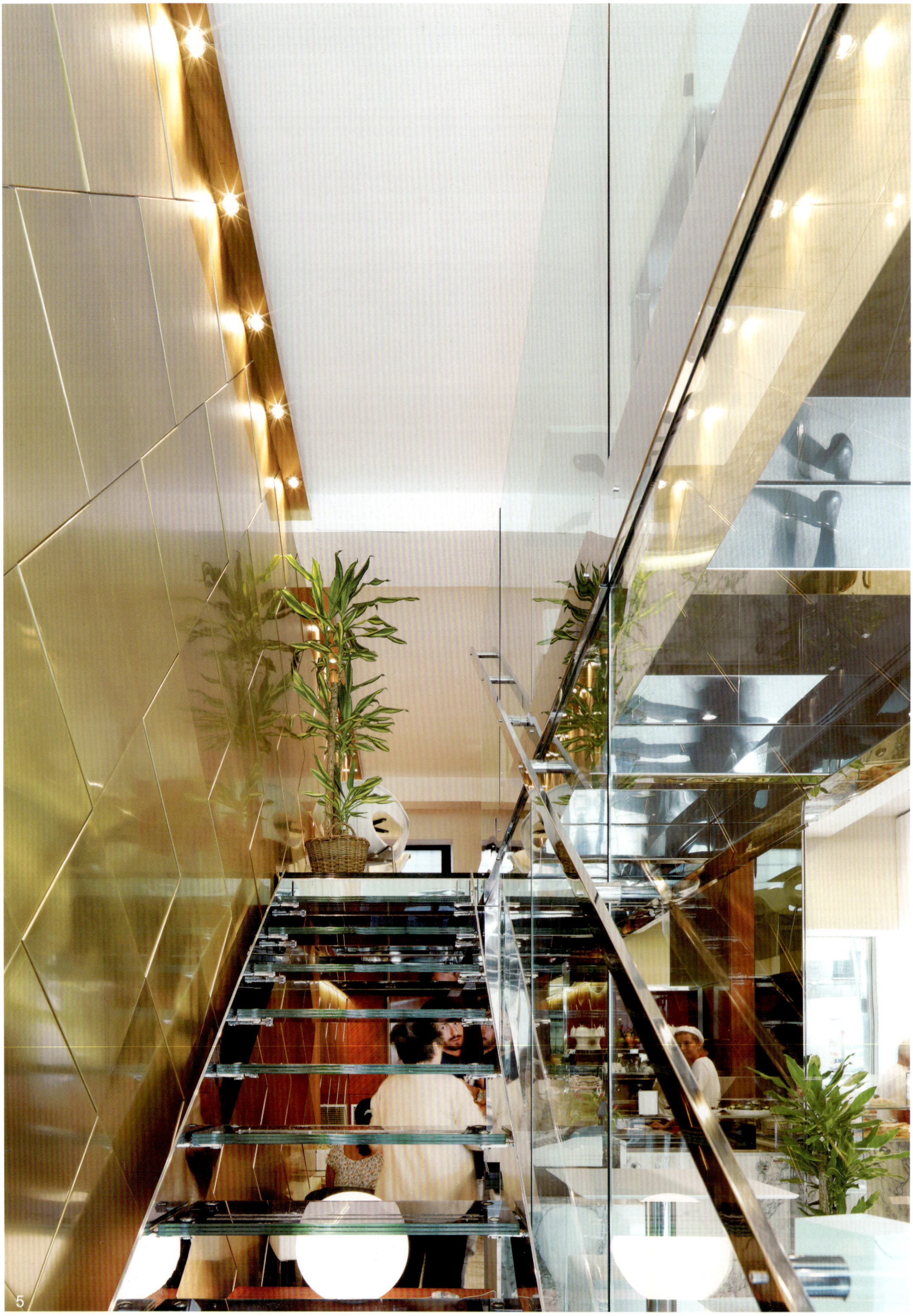

5

6

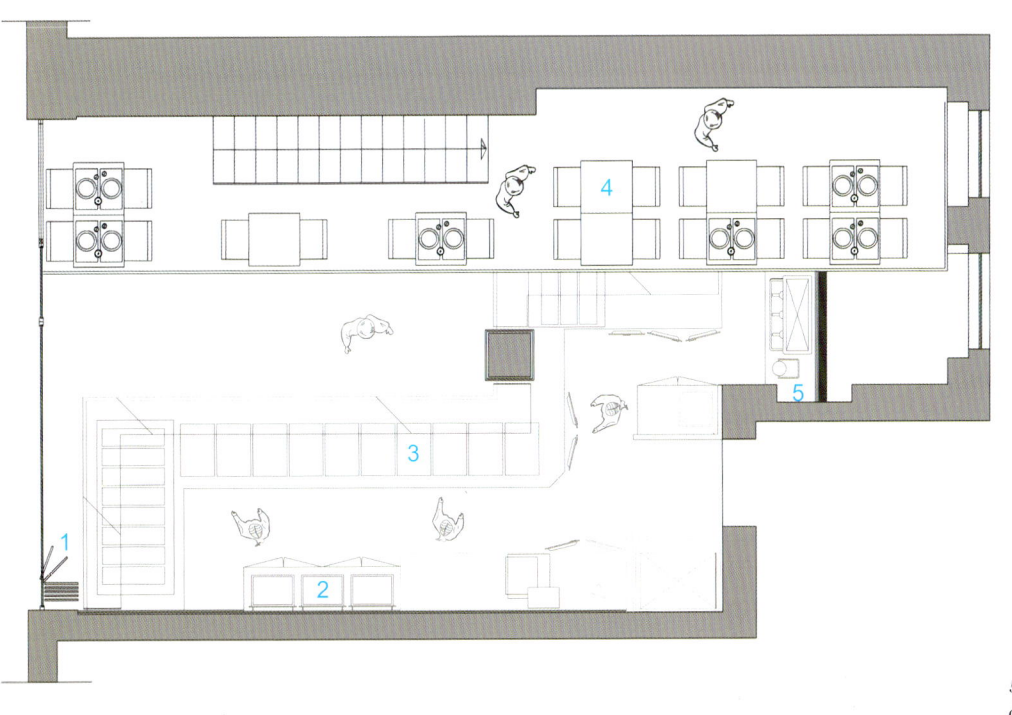

Floor Plan:
1. Entrance
2. Bread shelf
3. Counter
4. Seating area
5. Bathroom

5. Staircase leading to upstair dining area and the glass steps as the main feature
6. Upstair dining area: the golden wall, white ceiling and green plants creating a harmonious world

Chapter 3: *Holistic Design*

Giusto Gusto

Designer: Andrea Langhi
Location: Milan, Italy
Project area: 172m²
Project year: 2009
Photographs: Daniele Domenicali

In a historic building in the centre of Milan, the interior has been designed as architecture. Stucco, marble and glass emphasize the historical character of the inside of the building. Geometric designs in black glass and mirror, a ladder, steel and polished glass, which leads to the upper region, giving a modern twist.

The exhibited products, bread, pastry, ice cream, seem jewellery in glass cases while upstairs a backlit glass wall makes this area bright, modern and light. The monumentality of the rest of the room is in contrast.

The atmosphere created in this room is a mixture of strength and elegance. The materials used, such as marble, glass and steel were chosen for better definition of the monumental and the idea of modernity that inspired the designer.

Space switches from glass to marble, from the solid and strong to the soft colours and comfortable surrounding. The white walls, the shiny steel, the black glass and marble echo whispering softly are almost love poems. The modernity of crystal chandeliers and historical character of the columns in the back bench give to the local those detailed particularities that highlight even further the sinuous lines in space.

To the upper level the walls are transformed from a simple wall into a white glass wall that lights to the best the space available and allows customers to relax comfortably seated on chairs and sofas in soft white leather. The design is centred on the pursuit of luxury, not an end in itself, to give to the place a precise touch of taste and style. Combining the elegance of the design to the monumentality of the historical building in which it was designed, has been the guideline that led to realise a place of great visual and emotional impact.

2

Floor Plan:
1. Laboratory
2. Shop area
3. Staff restroom
4. Public bathroom

1. Shop area viewed from mezzanine
2. The charming chandeliers dangling from the ceiling and highlighting the products displayed in glass cases
3-4. The deep coloured marble counter and floor contrasting with the white ceiling and chairs along the French windows

111

5

5. Staircase leading up to the mezzanine
6-8. Dining area on the mezzanine emphasizing luxurious style and the logo on the wall adding playfulness

Chapter 3: Holistic Design

Callegaro

Designer: Andrea Langhi
Location: Milan, Italy
Project area: 148m²
Project year: 2008
Photographs: Daniele Domenicali

This is a dramatic interior, designed in black and white with a touch of metal gold polished. Modern lines mixed with some classical elements, such as the chandelier with glass pendants, the central column of stone and the original arches above.

The mirrors emphasize and embellish the space, while a curious upholstered bench welcomes guests as in an alcove that make the interior atmosphere even more charming and elegant. LED lights are reflected in the glass display counter and with their sparkle light brighten up the space evenly. The dark ceiling is reflected in the floor made of black ceramic tiles, and the tables in black plastic are the perfect link between the two layers that form an environment of warm tones and refined.

Attention is paid to the detail, furnishings and solid as well as to softness, marking a visual journey of well-defined meaning, making Callegaro a place to rediscover the pleasure of the mixture of the classical and the modern.

Entering this room customers immediately feel the sensation of a luxurious and elegant environment where it is easy to be fascinated by the glittering chandeliers with glass pendants, from classical elements such as the centre column of stone and modern elements such as glass and plastic.

114

Off White
Rustic tiva
wainscotach celine

1-2. The colours of white and black highlighting each other and defining the luxurious style of the space
3-4. Light shining from the ceiling brightening the space
5. Glass balls suspending above the display counter creating a dreamy background together with the charming luminaries

Mid Wood, Black Board colorful chalk, white Rustic Floor dark, Black Roof, warm colorful graphics, retro sign

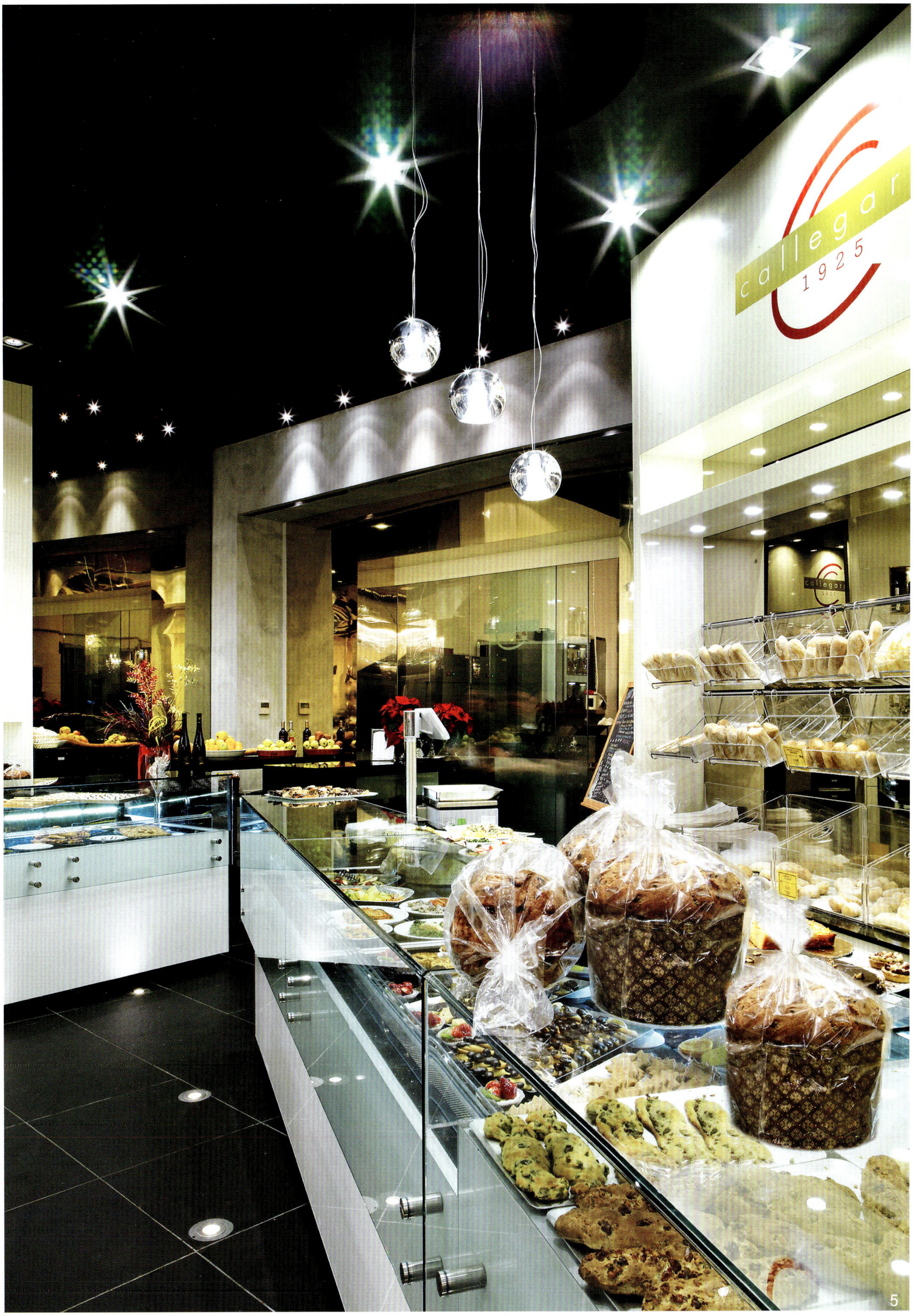

5

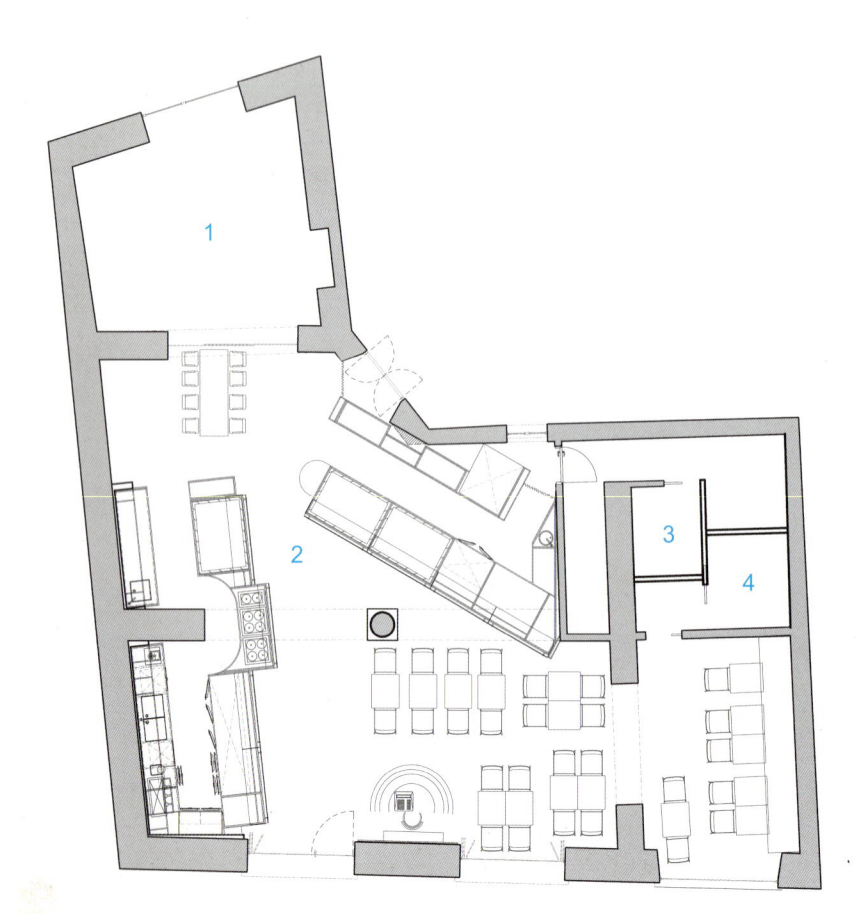

Floor Plan:
1. Preparation area
2. Display and dining area
3. Staff restroom
4. Public bathroom

6-7. The stone column and arches emphasizing classical style
8-9. The golden upholstered bench and chandeliers are really eye-catching.

Chapter 3: *Holistic Design*

Omonia Bakery

Designer: Bluarch Architecture + Interiors + Lighting, Antonio Di Oronzo
Location: New York, USA
Project area: 139m²
Project year: 2011
Photographs: ADO

This bakery is a brand new project for the family that owns the renowned Omonia brand famous for its Greek pastries. It sells pastries and breads prepared on premises in the see-through kitchen.

The design of this store celebrates indulgence – the suspension of the harsh reality of one's everyday grind through the consumption of a sweet delight. The space is soft and warm, sexy and decadent, as chocolate. Much like the physiognomy of a pastry, this design wants to offer the exciting anticipation of a pastry in preparation.

The space shifts organically with the narrative of flavours as patrons taste the succulent goods. The main feature of the interior space is a fluid surface (clad with chocolate brown Bisazza tiles) which covers the ceiling and the side walls to different heights. This surface warps in bubbles and negotiates a system of tubular incandescent light bulbs… and an arrangement of red cedar wood spheres. The epoxy flooring continues to the walls via filleted corners. A shelf and LED strips navigate the transition with the chocolate surface.

The exquisite level of craftsmanship needed to build the project with its unforgiving alignments and difficult details, is reflected in the exposed kitchen, which is simply sitting within a tempered glass box to show the artisanship of baking.

2

3

4

1-2. The bubbles dangling from the ceiling and illuminated by a system of tubular incandescent light bulbs
3-4. The chocolate brown Bisazza tiles wraps the ceiling and wall
5. Open kitchen in a glass box

Floor Plan:
1. Entrance
2. Service counter and display cases
3. Kitchen
4. Bathroom
5. Backyard

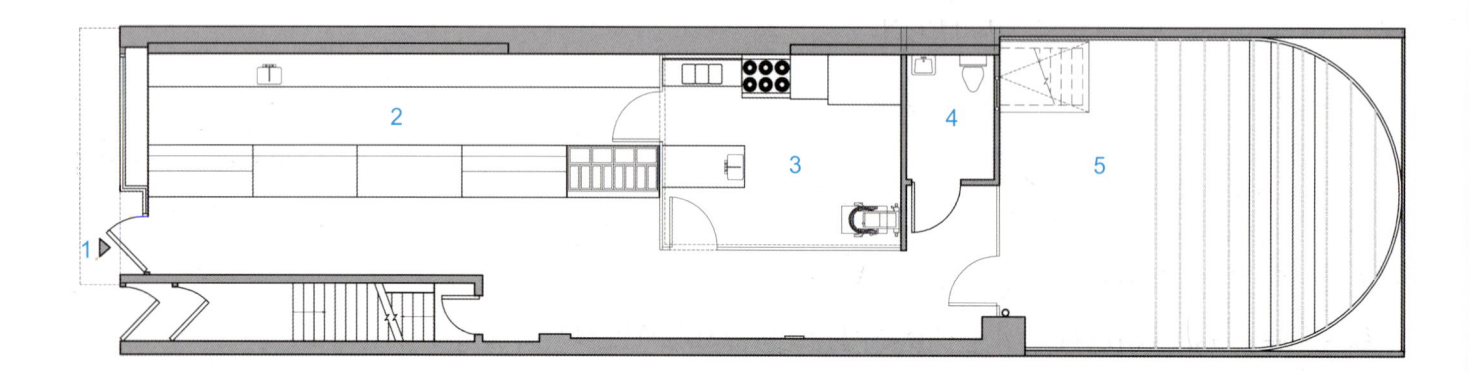

6-7. The main tone of the space reminiscent of baked products

Ceiling Plan

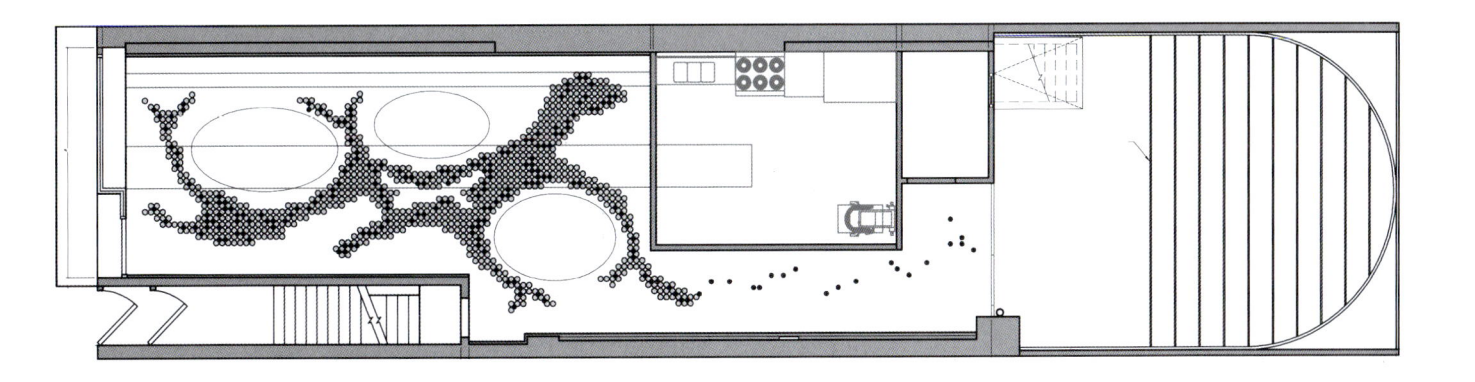

125

Chapter 3: *Holistic Design*

ODC BAKERY

Designer: Denis Kosutic
Location: Vienna, Austria
Project area: 66m²
Project year: 2010
Photographs: Lea Titz

This concept is dominated by a Mannerist reduction to the essentials. The large-sized, almost over-dimensional glass portal has been strictly reduced in terms of design. The boundary between the shop interior and the street disappears, while the shop opens itself up entirely towards the outside and actively participates in shaping the street scene with its complete interior. The broad range of products, reaching from the simple baguette to the most sophisticated patisserie products, has been translated into the interior design in an associative manner. What has resulted is a logical synthesis of products and merchandise carriers, which shape the room character not individually but only in combination with each other.

A few simple and very familiar materials provide the basis for the design. Just like the ingredients of a tasty marmalade recipe, these materials are processed only with a lot of care; the surfaces remain natural and untreated looking, just like a rough wall plaster or like polished wood slats.

The presentation furniture and merchandise carriers have been planned with high precision both in terms of functionality and design. Every irregularity and inaccuracy results from an exact planning process, in which the apparently faulty, accidentally resulting solutions and subtle technical details get mixed up and supplement each other in a balanced way. The design result emerges – thanks to its intended 'self-made' effect – from the focus of the main reflection, thereby becoming a natural component of the room design.

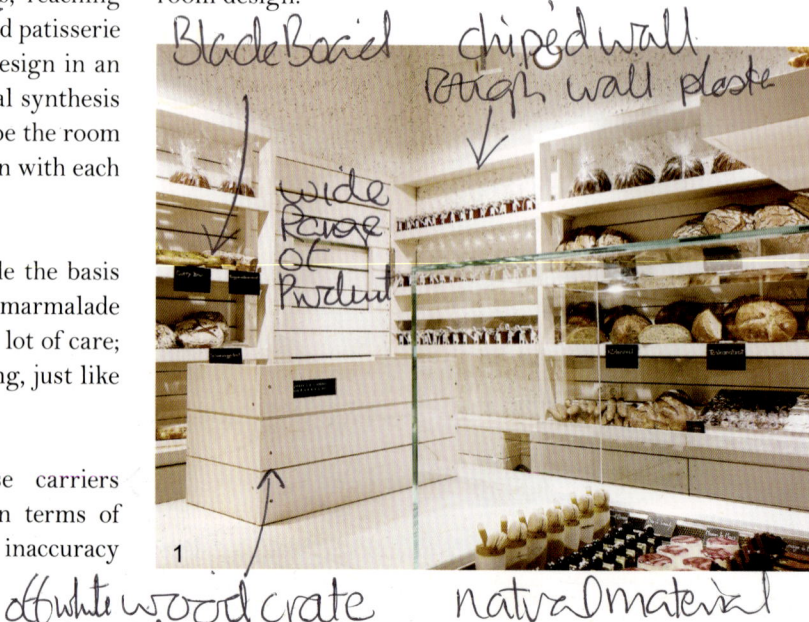

bright
neon
signage

basket

Bread Rustic
Food

Materials and furniture:
Portal: frameless glass portal with automatic sliding door
Floor: Pandomo
Walls: coarse plaster, white painted
Merchandise carriers: custom-made design; spruce varnished and polished
Vitrines: premimum steel with glass top
Merchandise illumination: custom-made design
Illuminated sign: neon
Luminous sign: three-dimensional, revolvable illuminated sign
Folding arm awning: fabric

frameless display

129

1. White as the main colour of the space
2. The red fabric folding arm awning adding a touch of brightness to the shopfront
3-4. The colourful baked products translating into ornaments of the space
5-6. The distinctive luminaries suspended from the ceiling

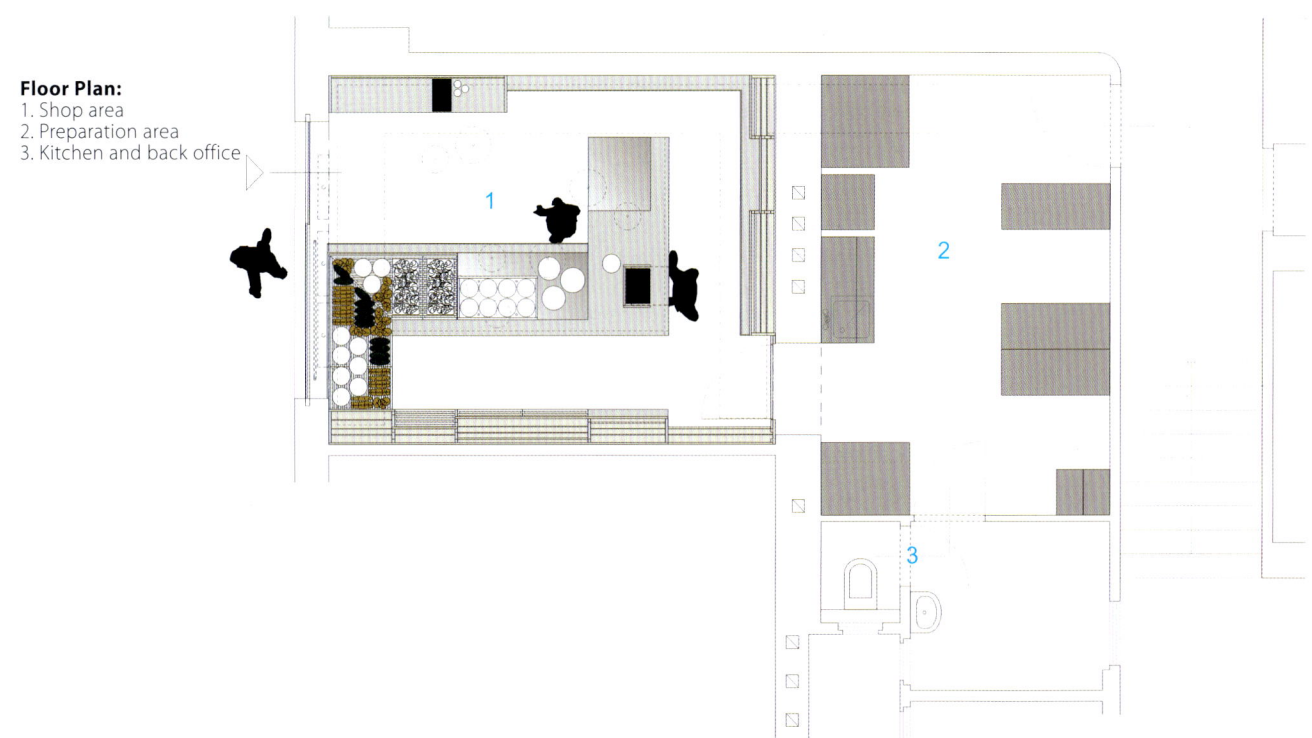

Floor Plan:
1. Shop area
2. Preparation area
3. Kitchen and back office

131

Chapter 3: *Holistic Design*

Orlando di Castello

Designer: Denis Kosutic
Location: Vienna, Austria
Project area: 420m²
Project year: 2009
Photographs: Denis Kosutic

The idea of uniting the worlds of Queen Elizabeth, the rapper 50 Cent and a girl from Tyrol all in one room and of forming from these associations, which are in contradiction to each other, a new kind of harmonic composition are the dominant factors of the outline. Symbols, such as delicate, stylised little flowers and hard metallic nuts appear in the room in countless versions, thereby making for strong contrasts.

The exciting sense of space appears through the examination of the new proportions: baseboards transform themselves into wall claddings; floor lamps become ceiling lights, panels of fabric divide into small note-like cloths; benches explode into small, kidney-shaped segments. The result of these alienations, often ironic, is a surreal atmosphere full of surprises.

White as the dominating room colour, freshly innocent and friendly, it has a differentiated and always different effect on various kinds of materials and surfaces. Being in a dialogue with metallic, silver and mirrored hard elements, the white colour repeatedly loses its innocence, thereby having a harder effect. On the other hand, the white background, immersed in warm light, shines with a smooth and golden warmness. The use of different kinds of seating furniture (shape but also seating comfort) in different room areas creates the intended space separation and zoning. The targeted use of illumination, as well as carefully planned and selected light colours support the atmospheres in particular areas.

The strong ODC branding appears to be dominant or reserved, characterised or printed on several custom-made objects and surfaces. Here, high-quality handicraft is in direct context with the quality of the brand 'Orlando di Castello'. In its distinctiveness, the architecture becomes the carrier of the brand development.

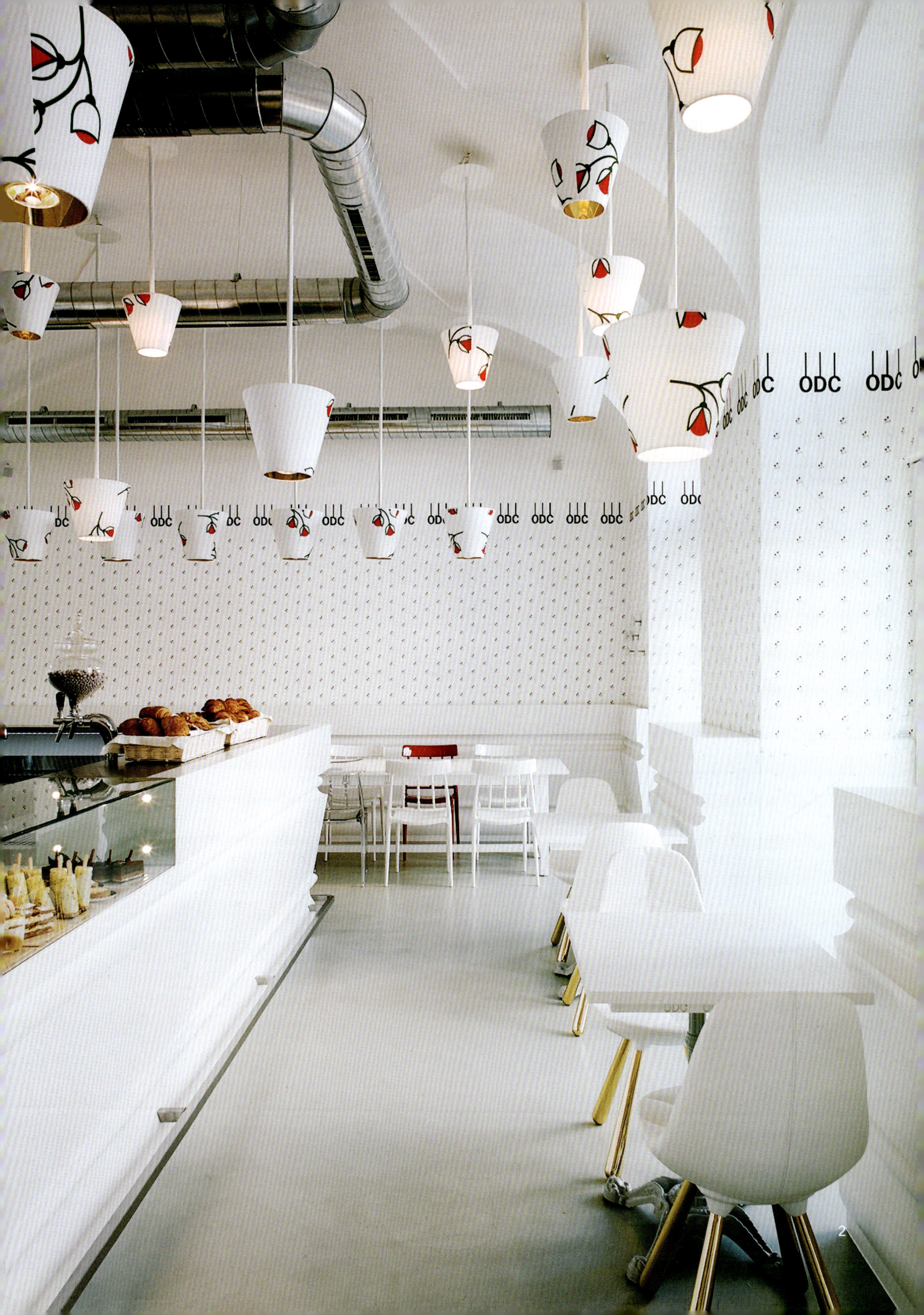

2

1. Shopfront viewed along the street
2. White dominating the entire room
3-4. The luminaries with red floral patterns creating a warm atmosphere
5. The dining area highlighting elegant feeling
6-8. Logos of the shop used as decorative element

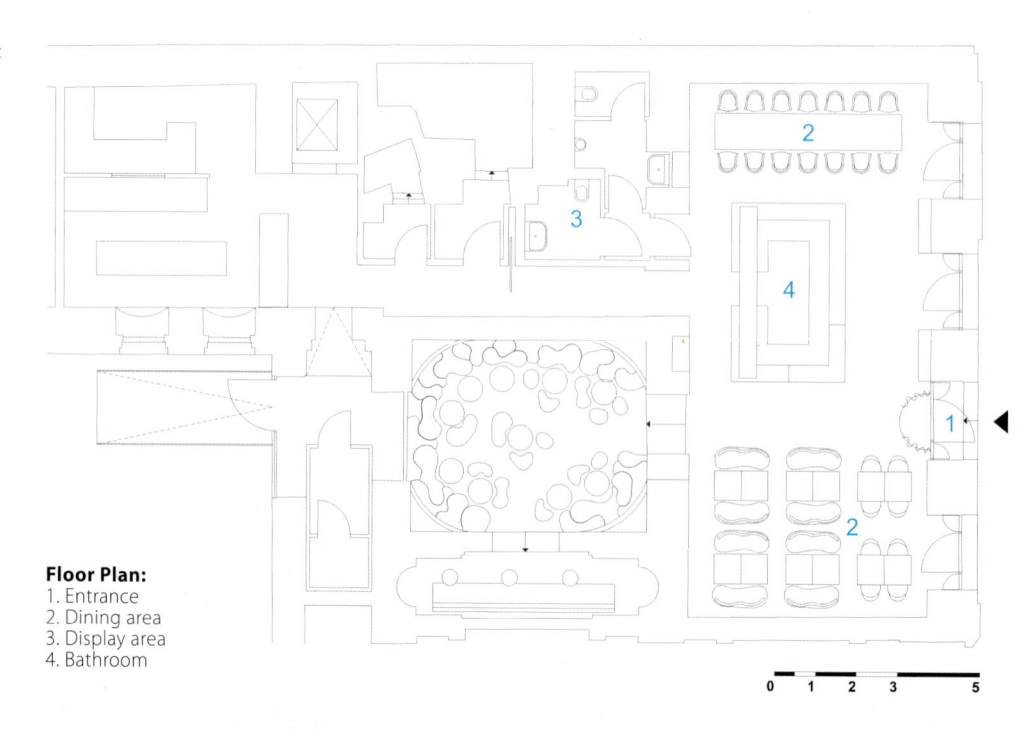

Floor Plan:
1. Entrance
2. Dining area
3. Display area
4. Bathroom

134

4

5

137

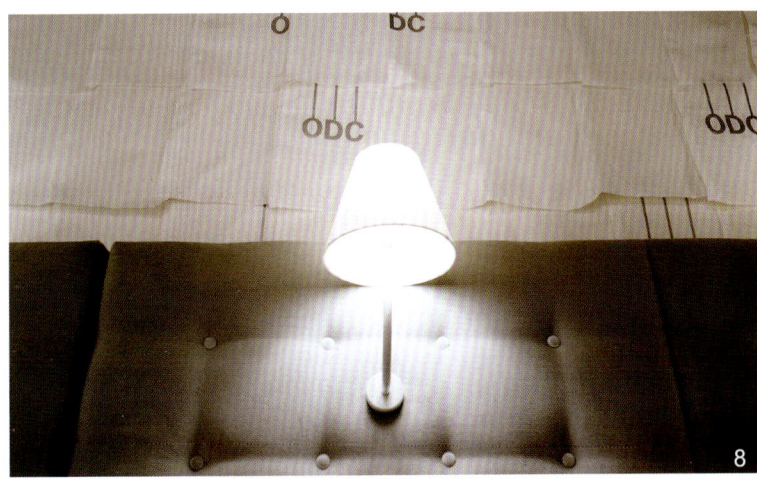

Chapter 3: *Holistic Design*

Helsinki Bakery

Designer: Arihiro Miyake/ Studio Arihiro Miyake
Location: Osaka, Japan
Project area: 200m²
Project year: 2008
Photographs: Potomak Co.,Ltd

The main concept is simple and modern interpretation of Finish fork-style. The space is composited dynamically with over 7-metre bar counter, long table and full glass showcase, yet natural wooden and white colour gives warm and clean impression. The wooden patch-work like façade is designed after Finish classic fork house covered with layers of birch plate. The furniture and their layout present the image of birch forest, and there is a motif of birch leaves drown on the walls which is only visible by lighting angles. The suspension lamps are originally designed to create the leaking light of wooden house.

The key idea for service is natural and health food; all dishes are Scandinavian traditional recipes and bread are made of rye wheat.

Helsinki Bakery

Helsinki Bakery
Shelve
<Market
movable for cleaning

3

Freta counte

full glass show case yet natural wood & white give warm & clean impressin

1. The shopfront boasting simple style
2. The tones inside in harmonious with the baked products
3-4. Wood as the main material and patterns of birch leaves on the wall emphasising natural feeling
5. Wooden patch-work like façade reminiscent of Finish classic fork house

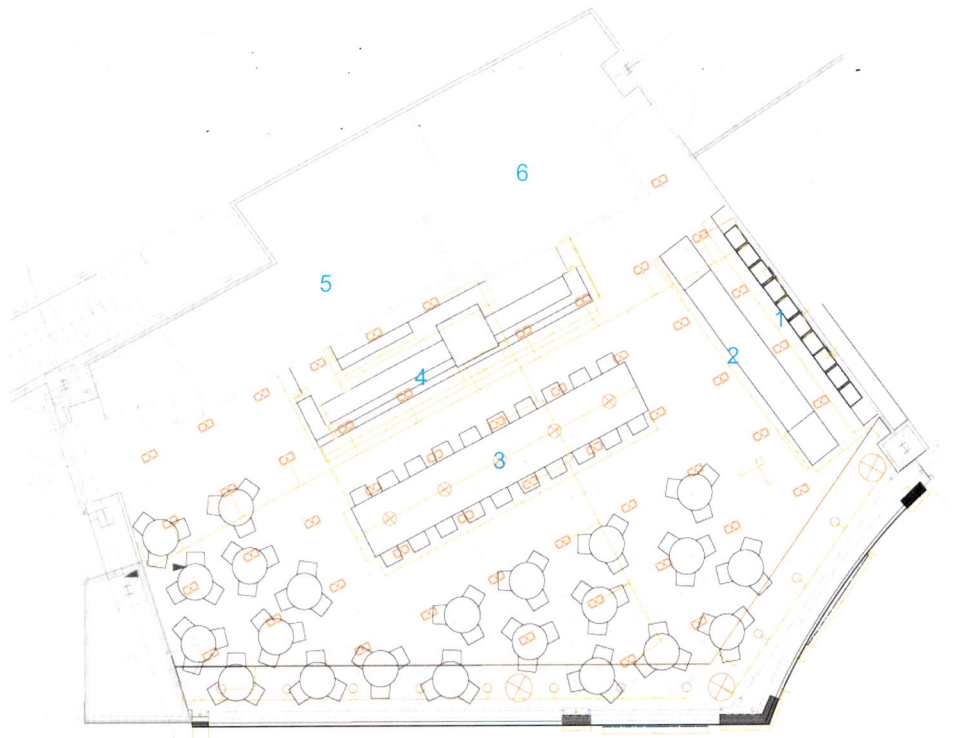

Floor Plan:
1. Bread shelf
2. Service Counter
3. Main Table
4. Bar Counter
5. Kitchen
6. Bakery

141

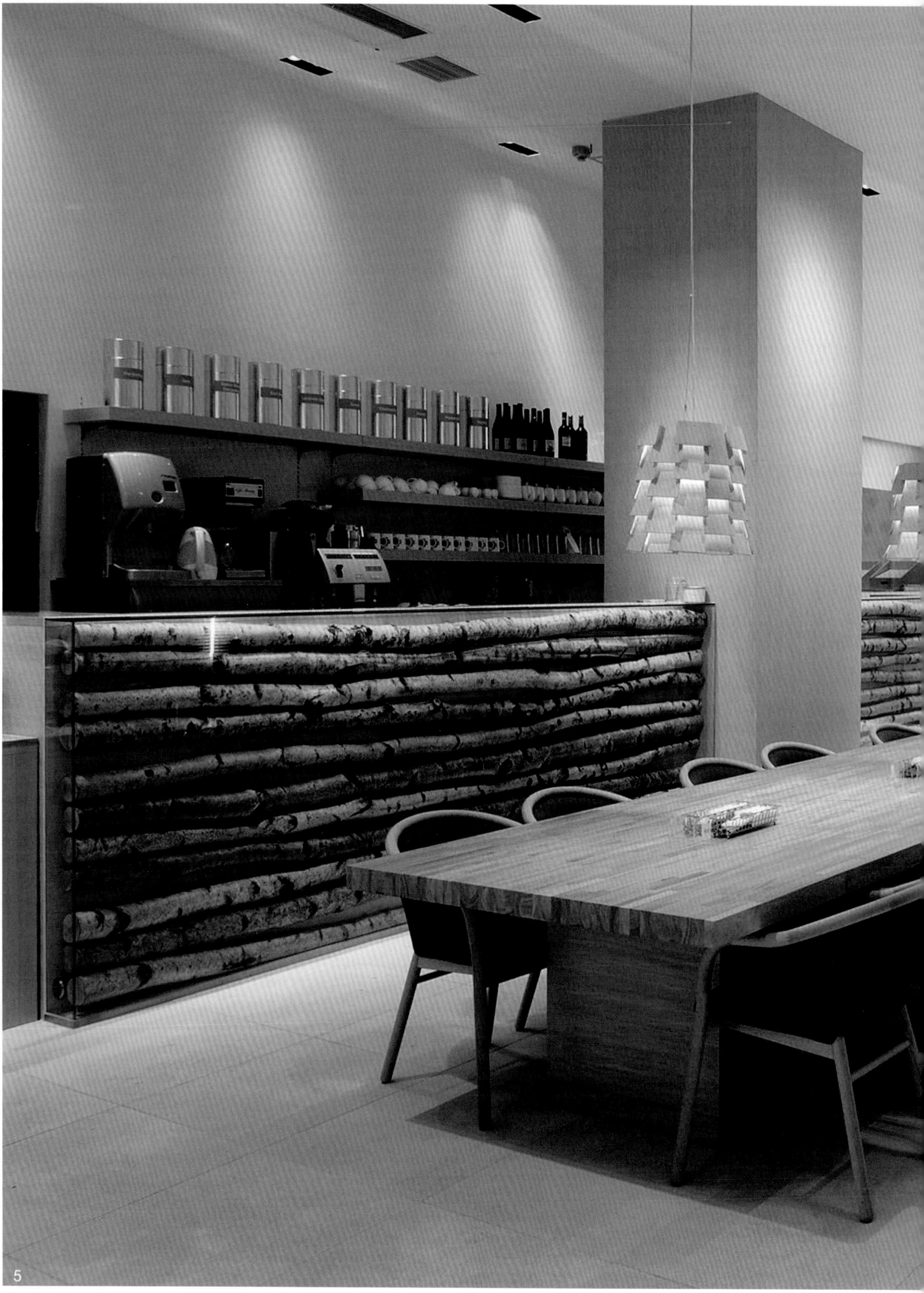
5

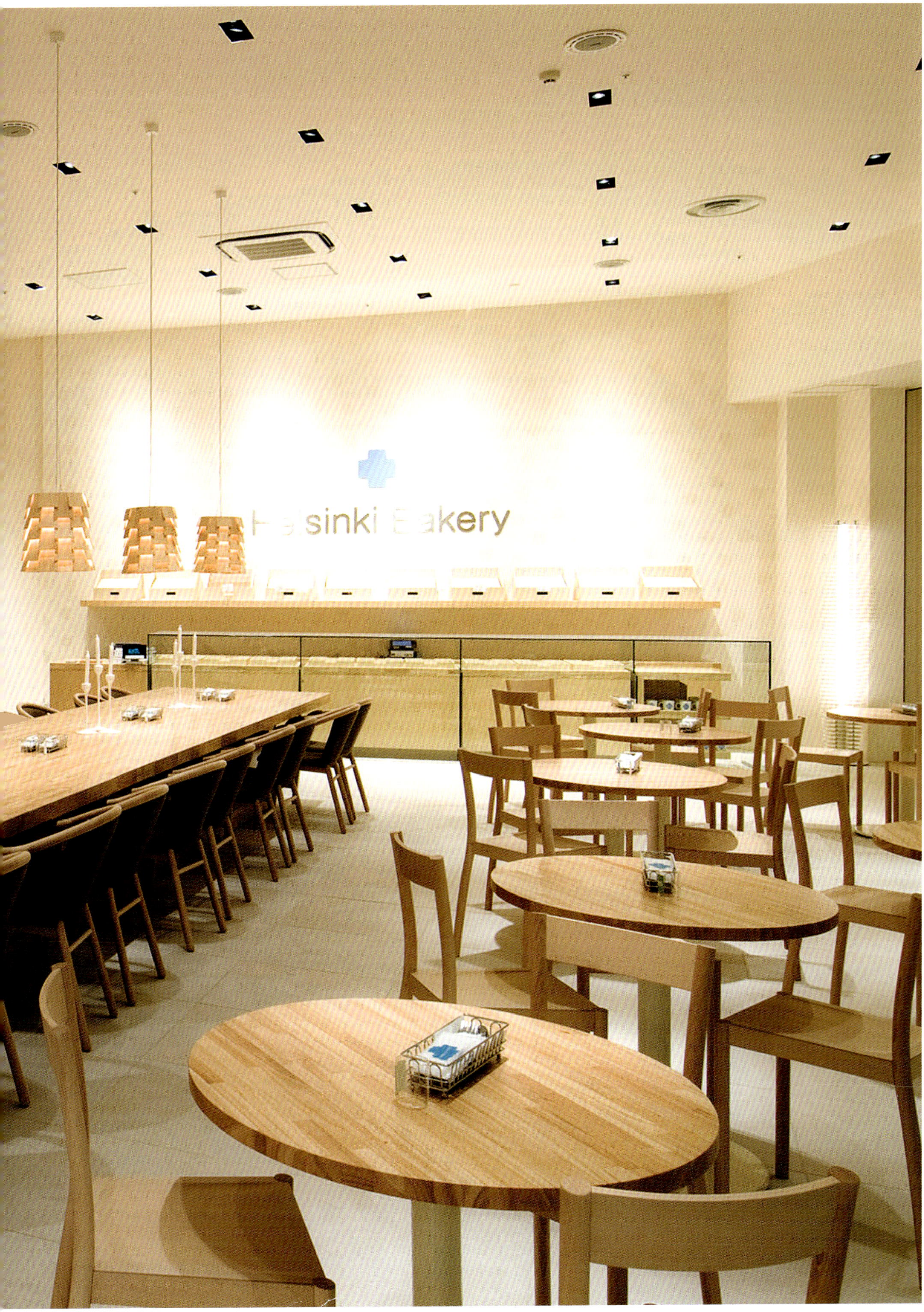

Helsinki Bakery

Chapter 3: *Holistic Design*

Sergio's Cake Shop

Designer: Forward Thinking Design
Location: Sydney, New South Wales, Australia
Project area: 83m²
Project year: 2010
Photographs: George Mourtzakis/TLP Studios, Barton Taylor, Barton Taylor Photographik
Shop flitter: Kalo Design

Sergio's Cake Shop is a family-run and Australian-owned company offering a lavish sensory experience of flavour in an opulent setting. Their luxurious cakes are hand finished and baked daily, recipes that have been tried and tested over decades, using the finest ingredients. They are delivered fresh daily to their franchises from their state of the art bake house kitchen.

Sergio's Cake Shop provides an intensely immersive brand experience. The design attributes much of its impact to the seamless integration of product, emotional associations with form and colour, and embodiment of the business's core values of quality and warm, friendly service. There is a strong level of simplicity and truth in the interior, which was drawn from the client being both retailer and manufacturer. The dark red tones of the environment make the client's passion for their offering tangible, and intensively evocative in engendering market loyalty and repeat response.

Sergio's is a surprising design, given its comparative opulence to its suburban central location, but it is exactly this uniqueness that makes the store imprint on the mind of today's aspirational shopper. Westpoint leasing are presenting the store as a flagship model of contemporary design.

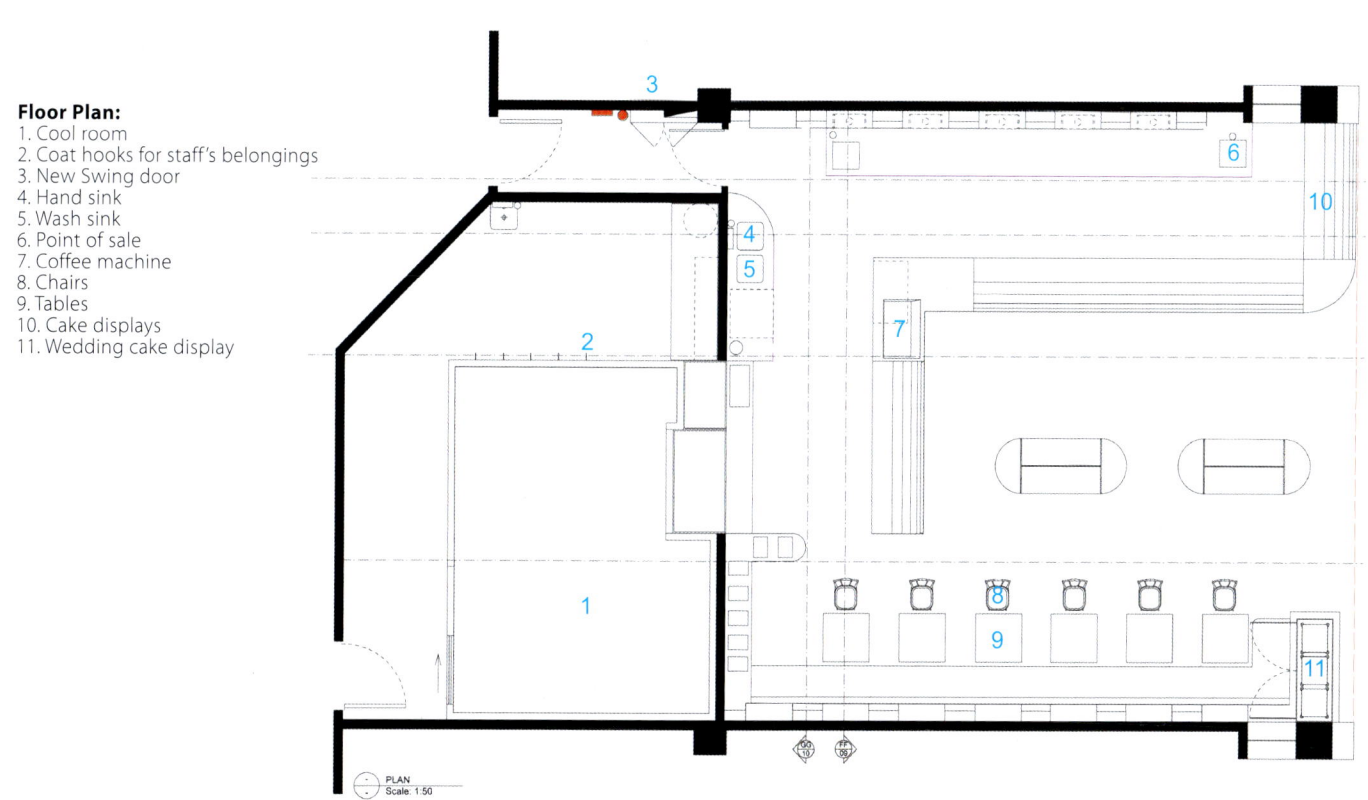

Floor Plan:
1. Cool room
2. Coat hooks for staff's belongings
3. New Swing door
4. Hand sink
5. Wash sink
6. Point of sale
7. Coffee machine
8. Chairs
9. Tables
10. Cake displays
11. Wedding cake display

145

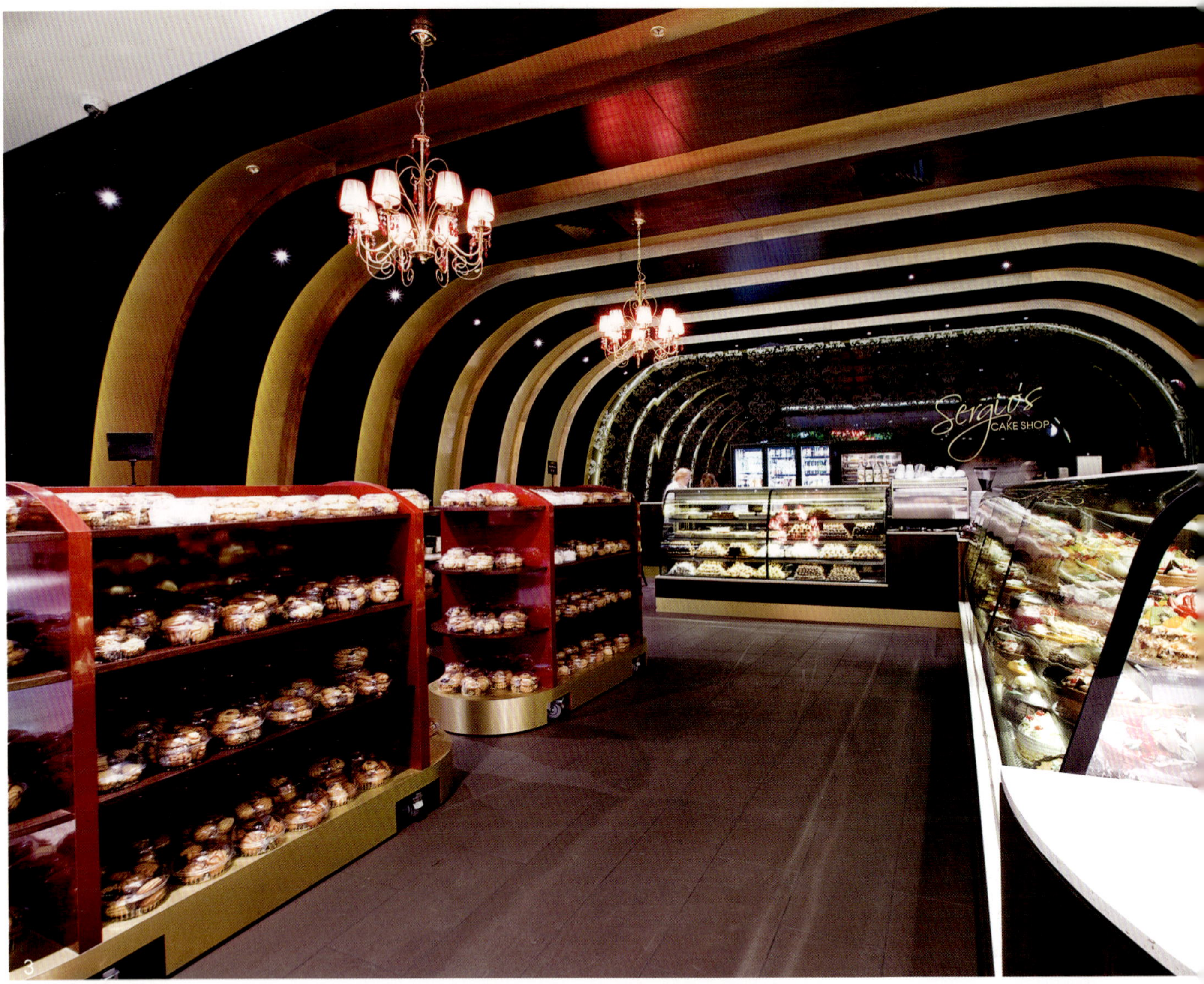

3

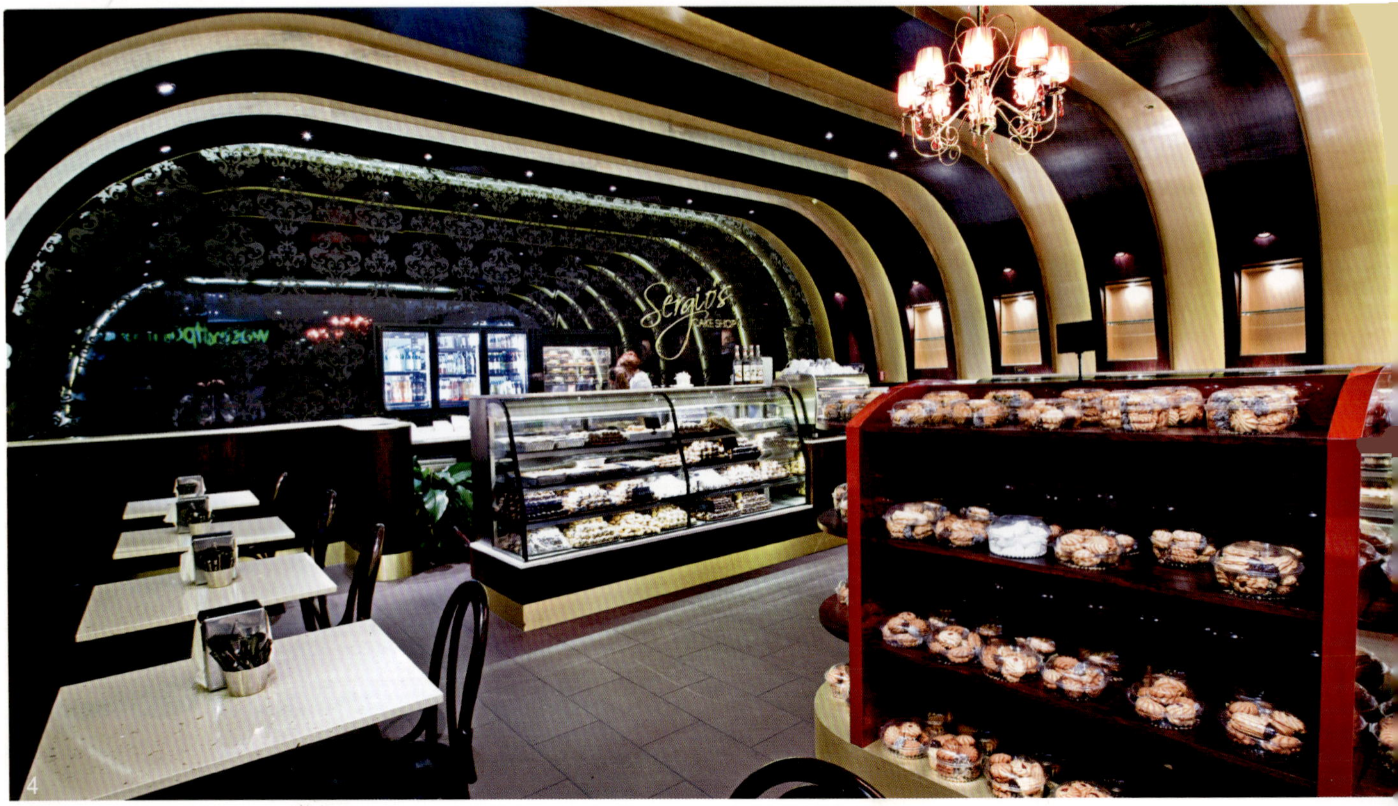

4

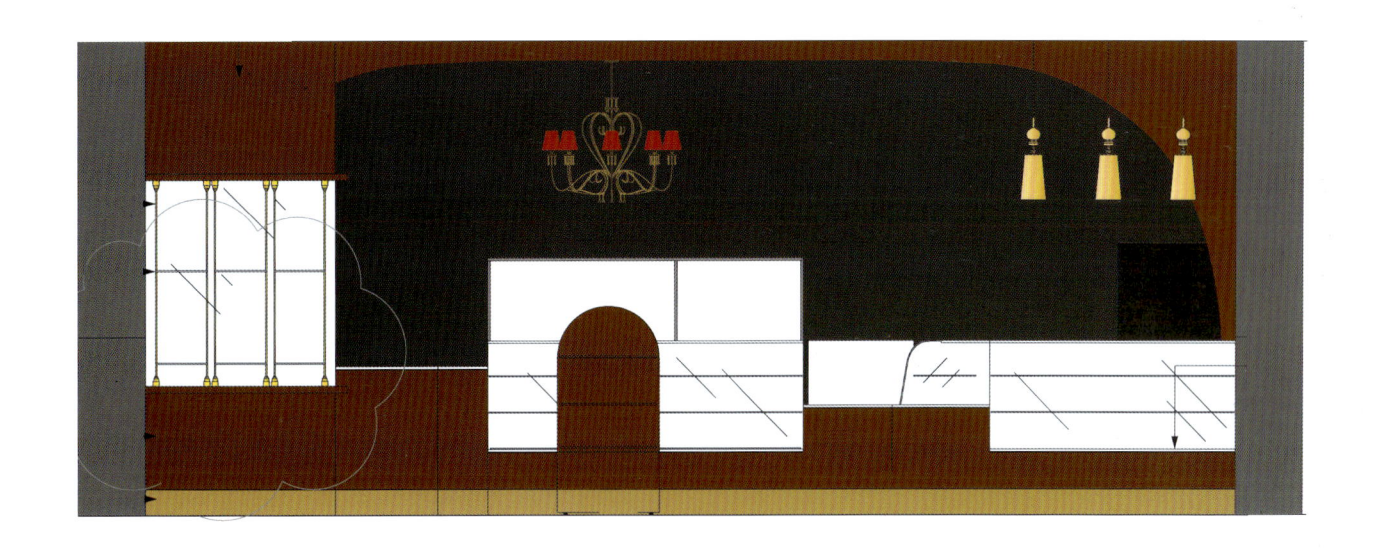

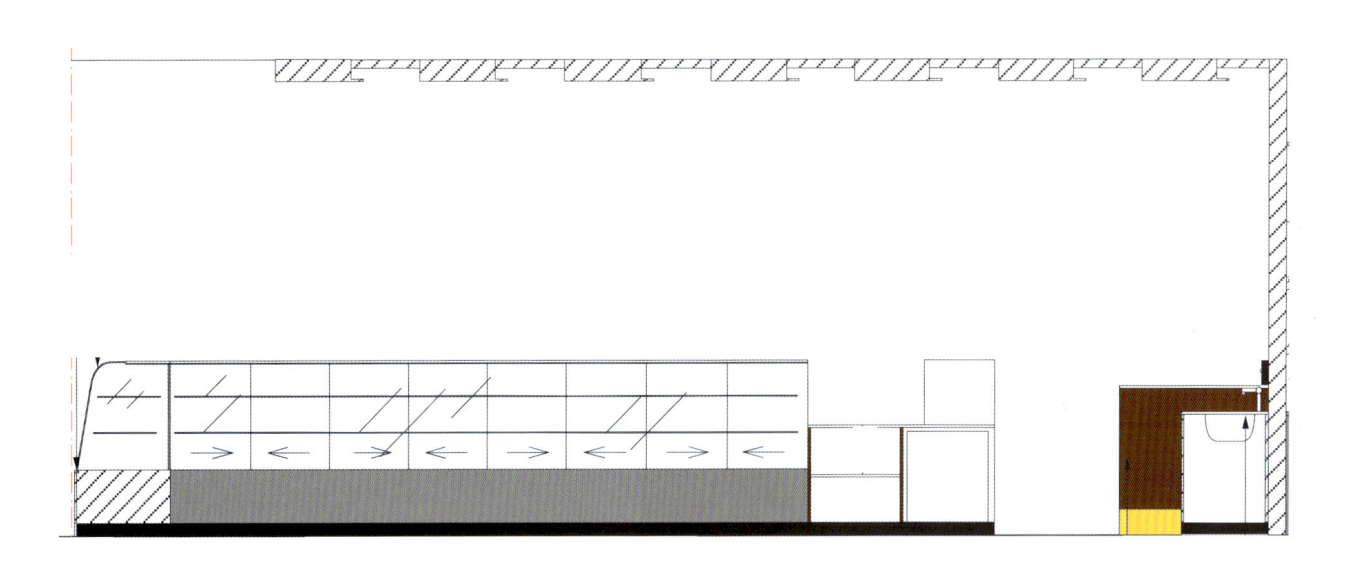

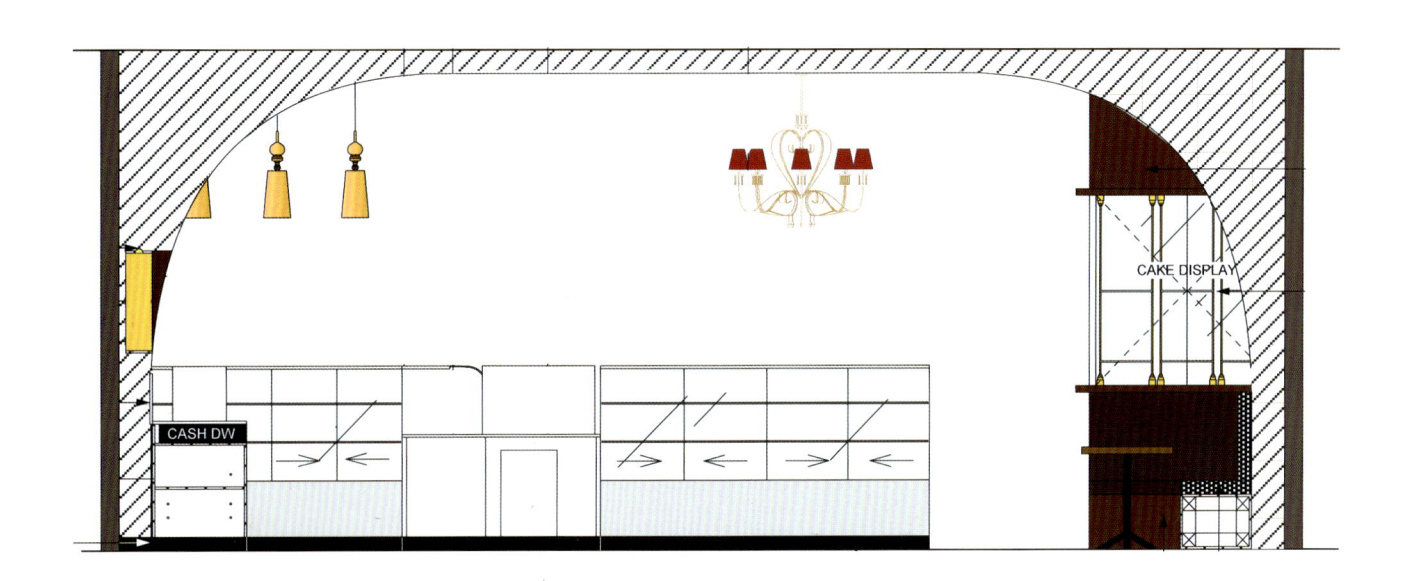

Elevations

147

1-2. Colourful products in the glass display case becoming decorative elements
3-4. The dark red tones creating a warm and cozy atmosphere
5-8. The yellow arches contrasting with the main colour and bringing touches of brightness

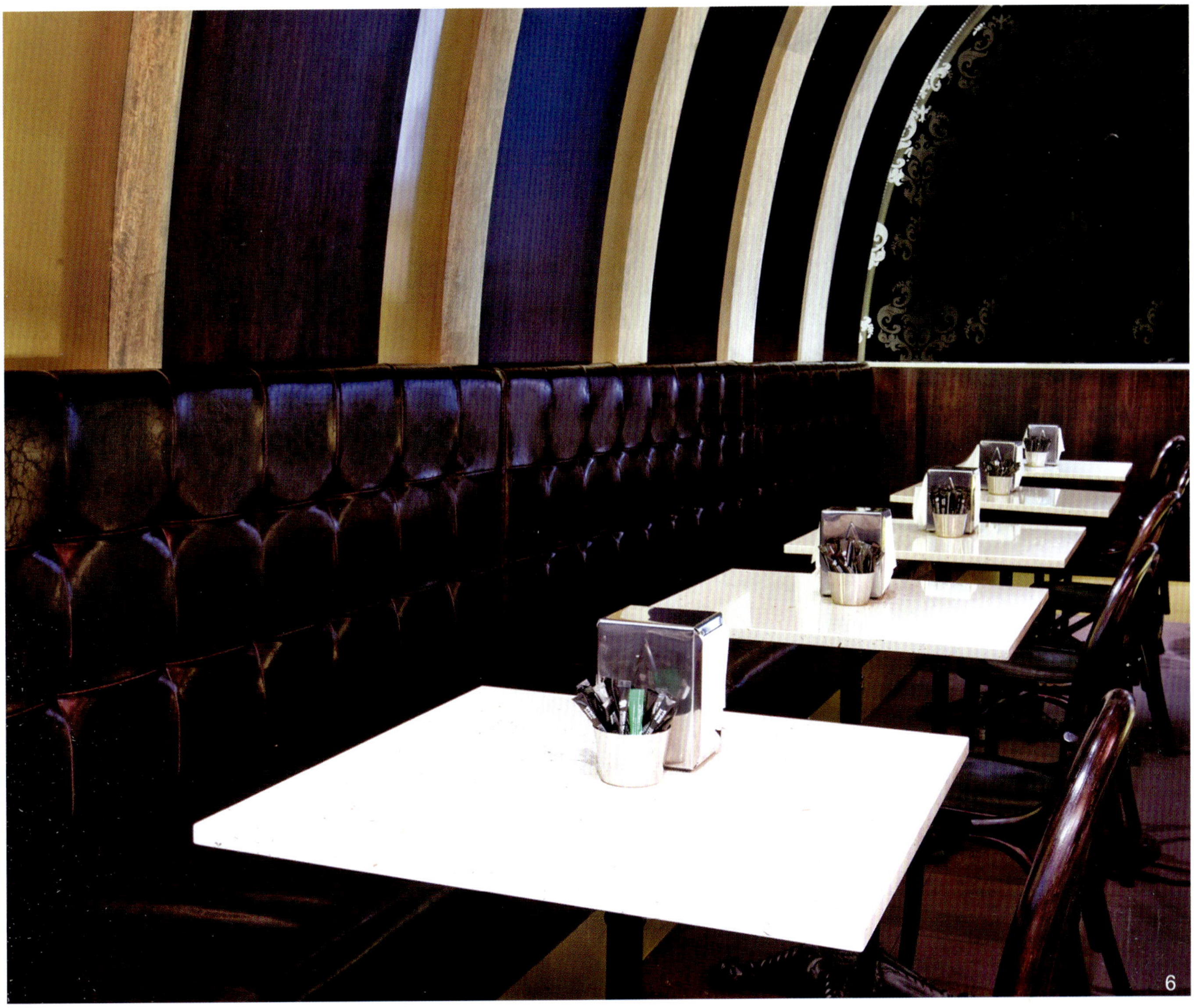
6

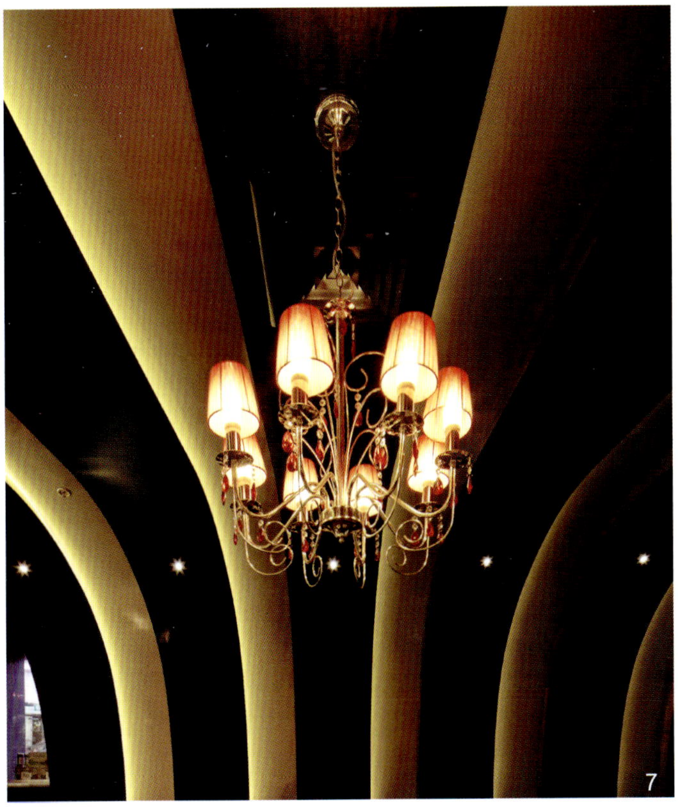
7

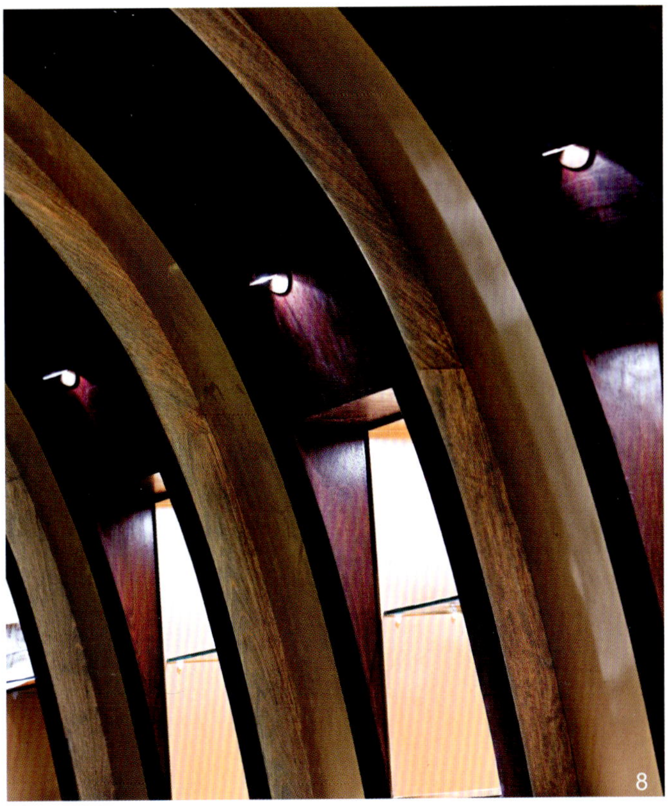
8

Chapter 3: *Holistic Design*

Sergio's Cake Shop Marrickville

Designer: Forward Thinking Design
Location: Sydney, Australia
Project area: 97.8m²
Project year: 2012
Photographs: Barton Taylor, Barton Taylor Photographik
Shop flitter: Kalo Design

Following the successful launch of their flagship store in Queensland Investment Corporation's Westpoint Blacktown, Sergio's Cake Shop set forth to bring their exquisite patisserie goods to another location - Marrickville Metro. Sergio's once again enlisted the services of Forward Thinking Design, the company who had envisioned and created the store design that is now synonymous with the brand. With the limitations of a much narrower space that was also exposed on three sides, the original layout could not be replicated. The solution was to divide the original plan straight down the middle to re-create the design in section.

After careful thought and consideration, the golden ribbed ceiling and warm timber tones were still able to be reproduced to create a space that reflected Sergio's persona: one of elegance, indulgence and opulence, whilst simultaneously being warm and inviting. The beautiful contrast of colours, decorative patterned walls, and delicate chandeliers produce a stunningly unique setting that allows the Marrickville store to stand out in its suburban shopping centre location.

Peter Christou, the owner of Sergio's Cake Shop, relates: 'Off the back of the success we are enjoying with Sergio's Cake Shop at Blacktown, and we are now franchising the business and rolling out the design across all future premises. Marrickville is our second store and the design has gone from strength to strength'.

1

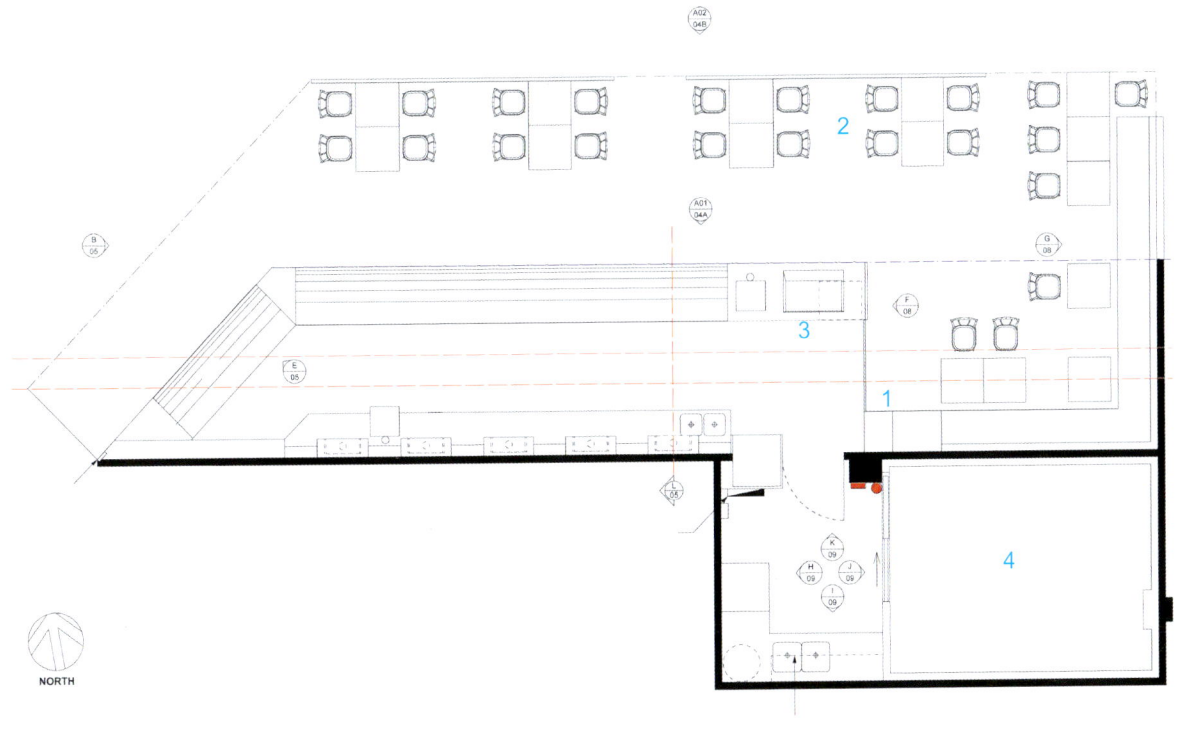

Floor Plan:
1. Display area
2. Dining area
3. Coffee bar
4. Cool room

151

1-2. The golden ribbed ceiling and warm timber tones embodying Sergio's identity
3. The floral patterned walls creating an elegant background for colourful products and contrasting with the bright yellow colour

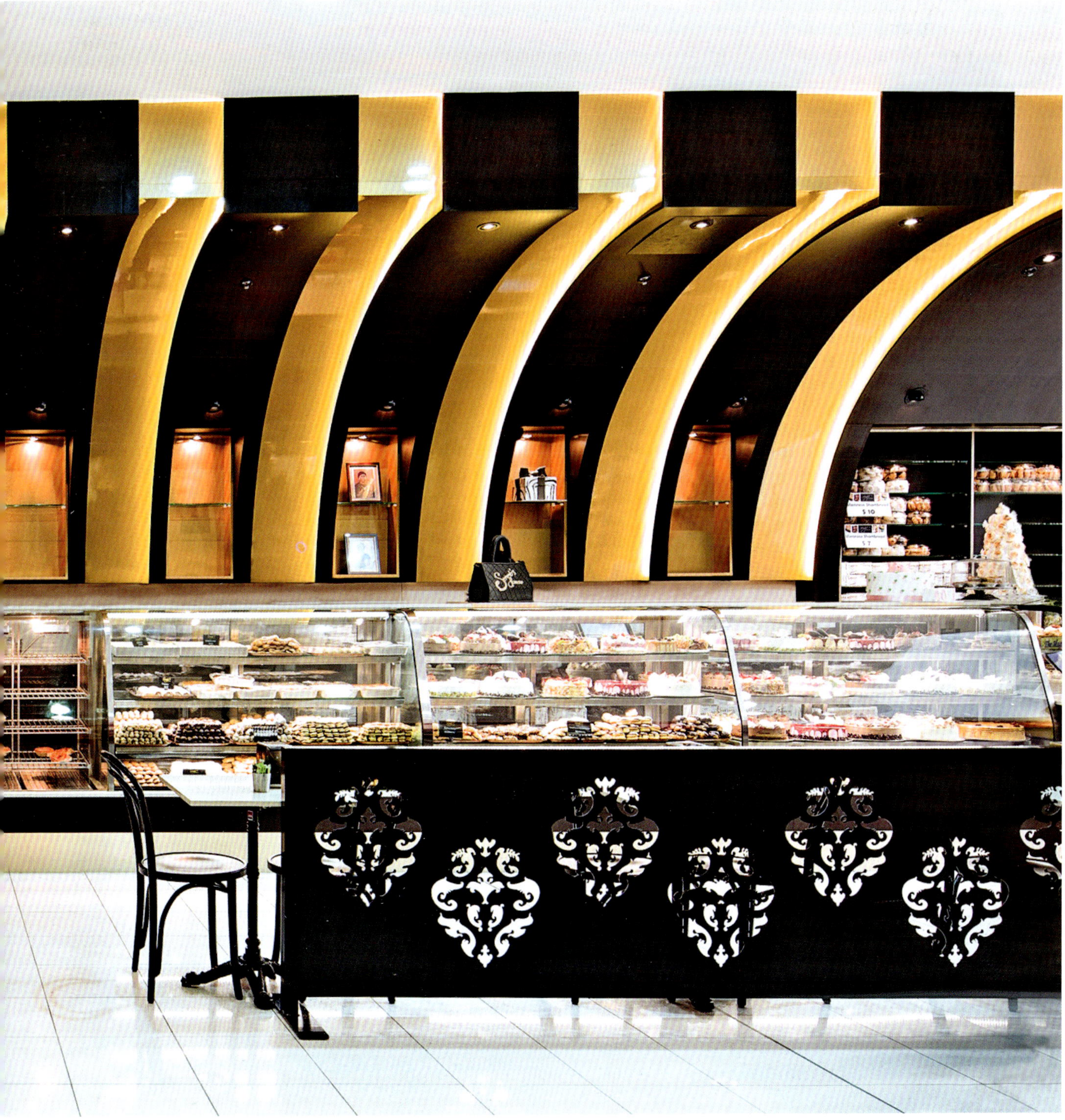

4

4-5. The delicate chandeliers brightening the whole space and bringing luxurious feeling

Chapter 3: *Holistic Design*

Vyta Boulangerie Italiana

Designer: COLLIDANIELARCHITETTO
Location: Turin, Italy
Project area: 150m²
Project year: 2011
Photographs: Matteo Piazza

Vyta Italian Boulangerie offers the oldest and most traditional food product, bread and its derivatives, in one of the most representative places for our society, Porta Nuova Train Station, the symbol of Turin's hectic urban life. 'Through simple products offered by Nature, such as water, wheat and fire, thanks to Man's expert hand, patience and creativity, forms, savours, and fragrant flavours have been created for millennia, giving birth to bread, ancient and modern nourishment for manhood.' This food philosophy was the starting point that inspired the architectural concept.

A contemporary look has been reformulated for the most 'minimal' product on our tables. It originates from a restraint design and an innovative, cool elegance, the result being a sophisticated minimalism and a formal reduction to the essential. The project features contrasting materials and colours: oak and corian as representatives of tradition and innovation, an integration of nature and artifice. The juxtaposition of soft oak and black declined in its various material aspects creates an exclusive, theatrical environment, where the warmth of the natural texture is enhanced by the contrast with glossy black surfaces and volumes. These come up as large ceramic tiles on the floor, corian for the counter and black polymer for all the vertical panels that fold the space like in a treasure chest. The hood is one of the most significant components of the setting, due to the shape and size of its natural oakwood planks that evoke the interweaving of traditional bread baskets. This volume has been brought down to a human architectural scale, so that the space has a less monumental and more intimate look. The rosette, a typical breadshape that was mainly consumed by workers in 1700, has been manipulated into a three-dimensional pattern in an oversized version: as an oakwood element it overlaps and repeatedly comes up until it fades against a glossy black polymer background. As a mirror panelling it completely lines the space and transforms it into a kaleidoscope of endless reflections that creates an ever-changing environment. The light system contributes to soft and intimate atmospheres: it diffusely radiates on the counter, enhances the hood and the rosette elements by means of recessed metal halide light sources by IGuzzini; it is an eye-catcher above the tables thanks to sculptural Tropic Bell lamps by Foscarini; it gets highly technological to celebrate bread and its derivatives through a cluster of LED s.

The custom-designed hexagonal tables sport a shape and distribution that refer to the pure geometry of beehives. At the same time the ensemble evokes the ancient rite of eating together, a less common practice nowadays, but increasingly necessary in the third millennium's life.

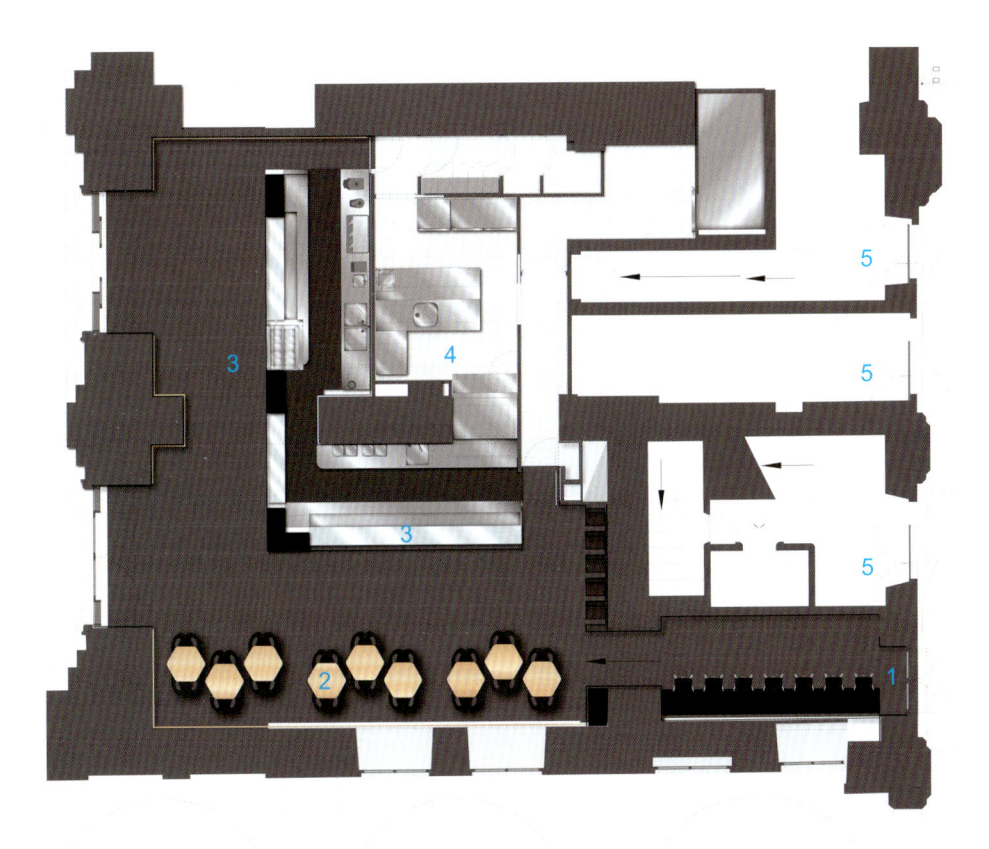

Floor Plan:
1. Entrance
2. Dining area
3. Display
4. Kitchen
5. Staff access

157

2

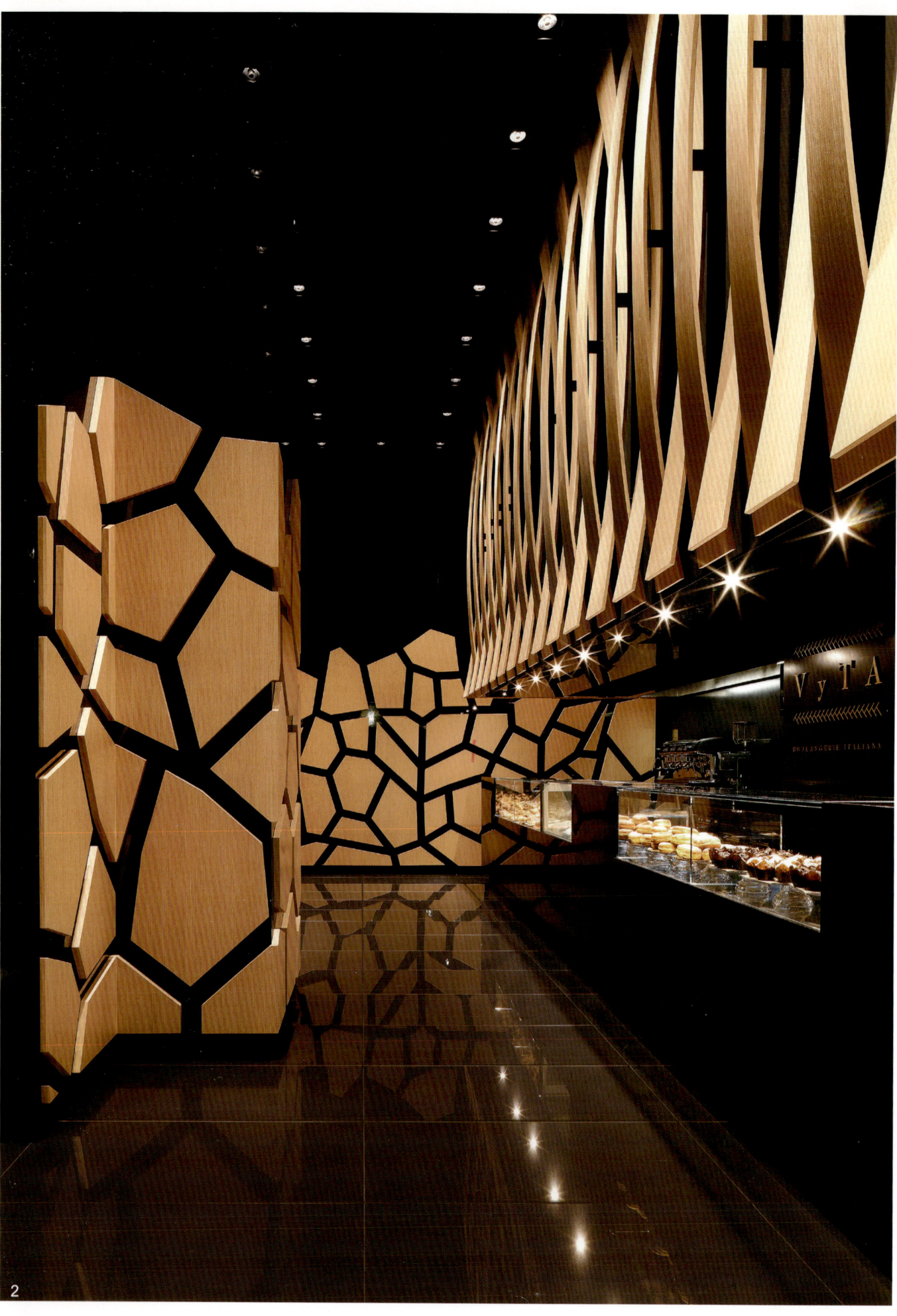

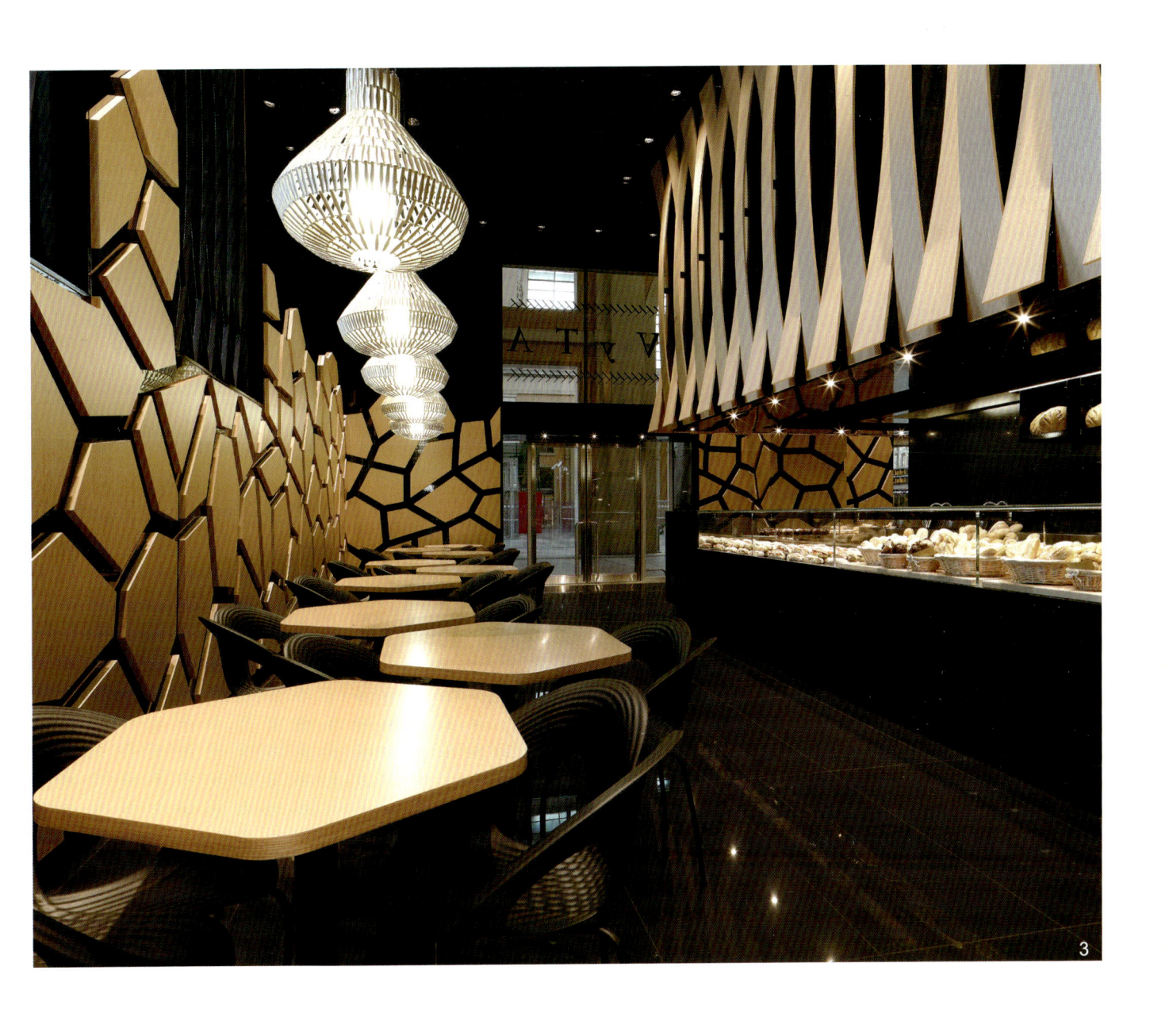

1. Shopfront view
2-3. Natural oakwood planks and black surface contrasting each other and forming together a luxurious space

159

4-5. The lighting system contributing to soft and intimate atmospheres

Drop with stay

Sections

5

Chapter 3: *Holistic Design*

Sweet Alchemy Pastry Shop

Designer: Patsiaouras Nikos, Marielina Stavrou, Nikos Patsiaouras
Location: Athens, Greece
Project area: 96m²
Project year: 2012
Photographs: Giorgos Sfakianakis

The store is located in the upmarket suburb of Kifisia in the northern region of Athens. The client is Stelios Parliaros who is considered to be the best Patisserie in Greece, author of many culinary books and host of a very popular patisserie show in Greek TV.

Alchemy's notion associated with darkness mystery and mysticism is practiced in laboratories full of peculiar enigmatic devices, rare distils crystals and potions. These images were the starting point for the development of a central idea, the recreation of this atmosphere in a contemporary outtake.

The space is characterized by the high degree of transparency which was manipulated in order to diffuse the light and filter the optic penetration. The role of light was highly regarded and thoroughly studied since the beginning in order to create a unique solution for the particular location and user. Light and shadow change throughout the day giving the space a unique atmosphere every moment. Serenity is followed by tension and drama.

The punctured bronze skin of the main façades creates the impression of the chamber of treasures, of the golden cage which encloses the precious, the rare commodity, the sin of the pleasure of the forbidden fruit.

The philosophy behind the choice of materials was in tune with the philosophy of the client: selection of the raw materials and no substitutes. Iron, bronze, copper and wood were selected for their natural characteristics and were only processed but did not alter for an emulate appearance.

The purpose was not the stenographic representation of a mystic environment but the formulation of the spirit of the place, the 'genius loci', the atmosphere that would saturate the space and would transform it to a true place with its very own distinctive character. The sense of mythical, the mysterious discovery and the transition to another reality are the characteristics of the 'Sweet Alchemy' of Mr. Parliaros which the designers wanted to transfuse to the new store.

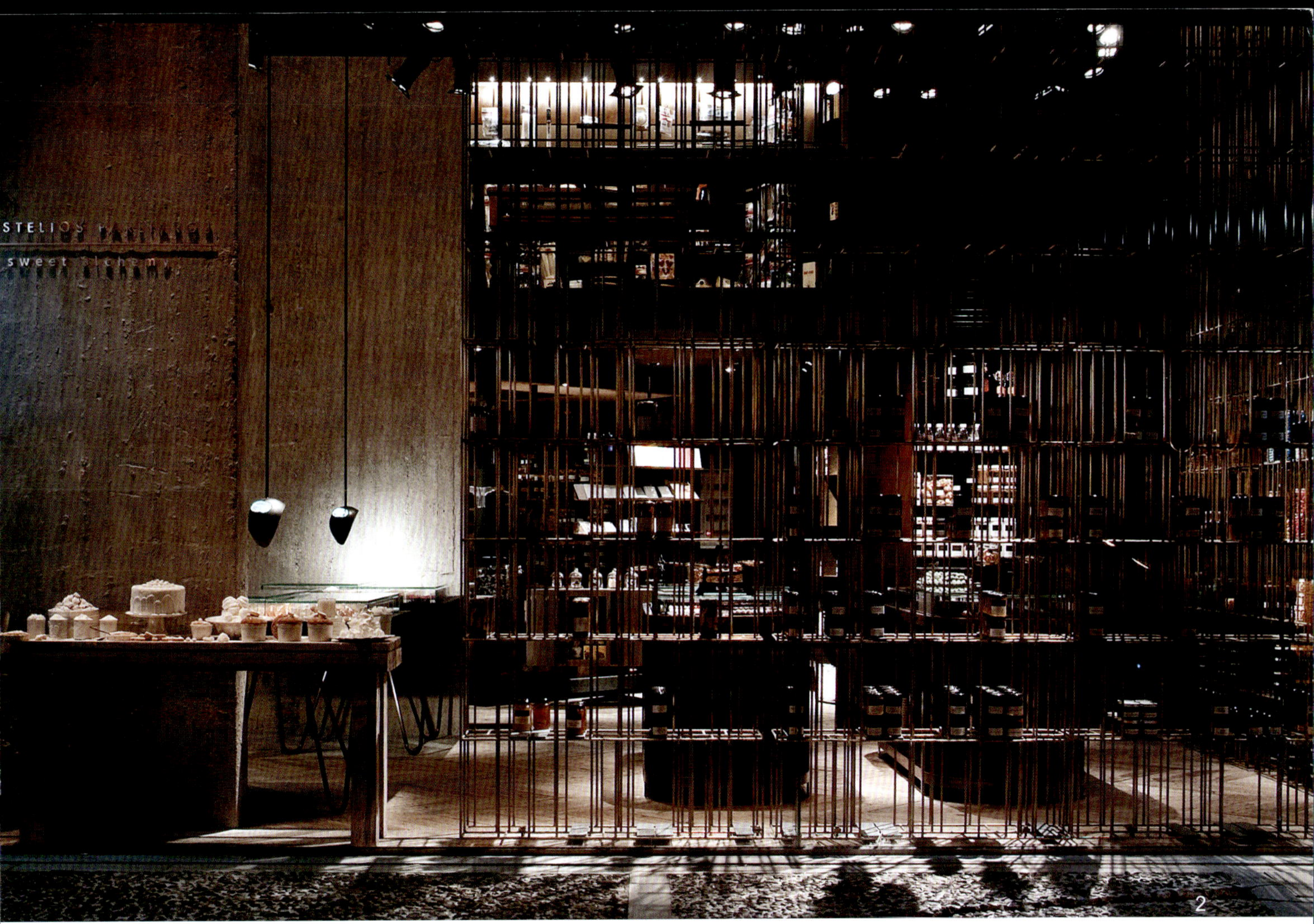

2

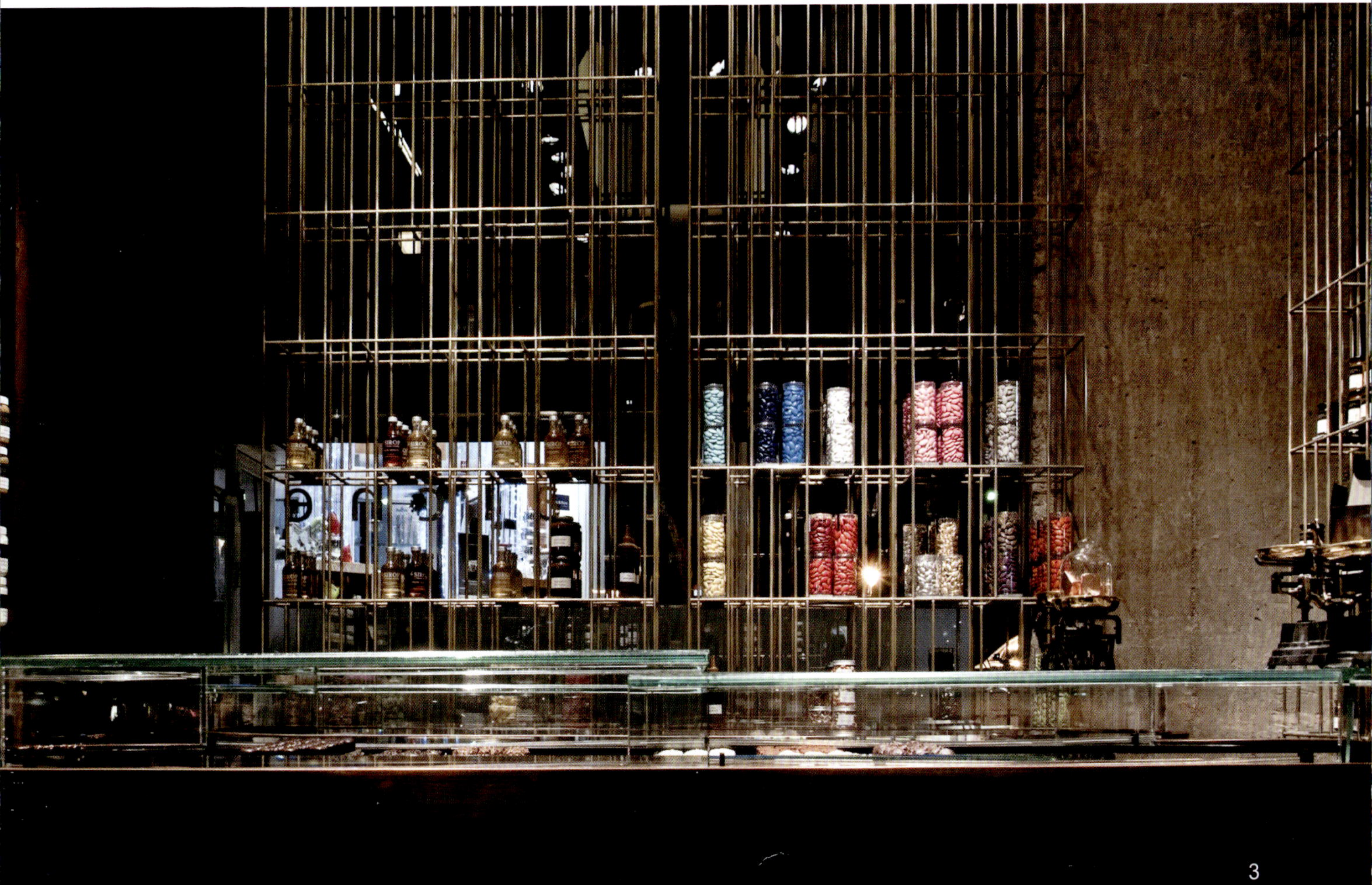

3

1-3. The dark tones boasting a mysterious feeling
4-5. Raw materials such as iron, bronze, copper and wood were selected to create a natural space.

Floor Plan:
1. Entrance
2. Cashier
3. Stairs
4. Display area

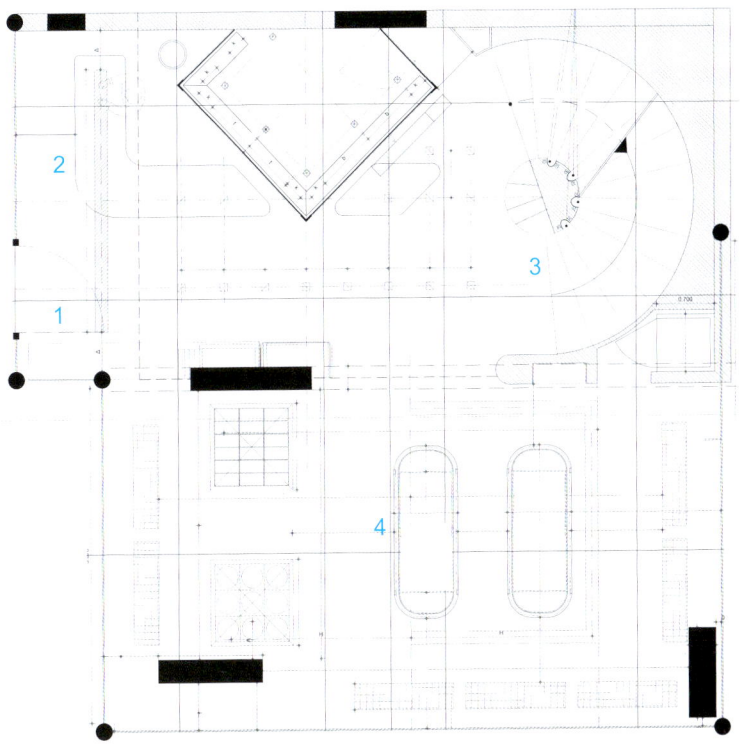

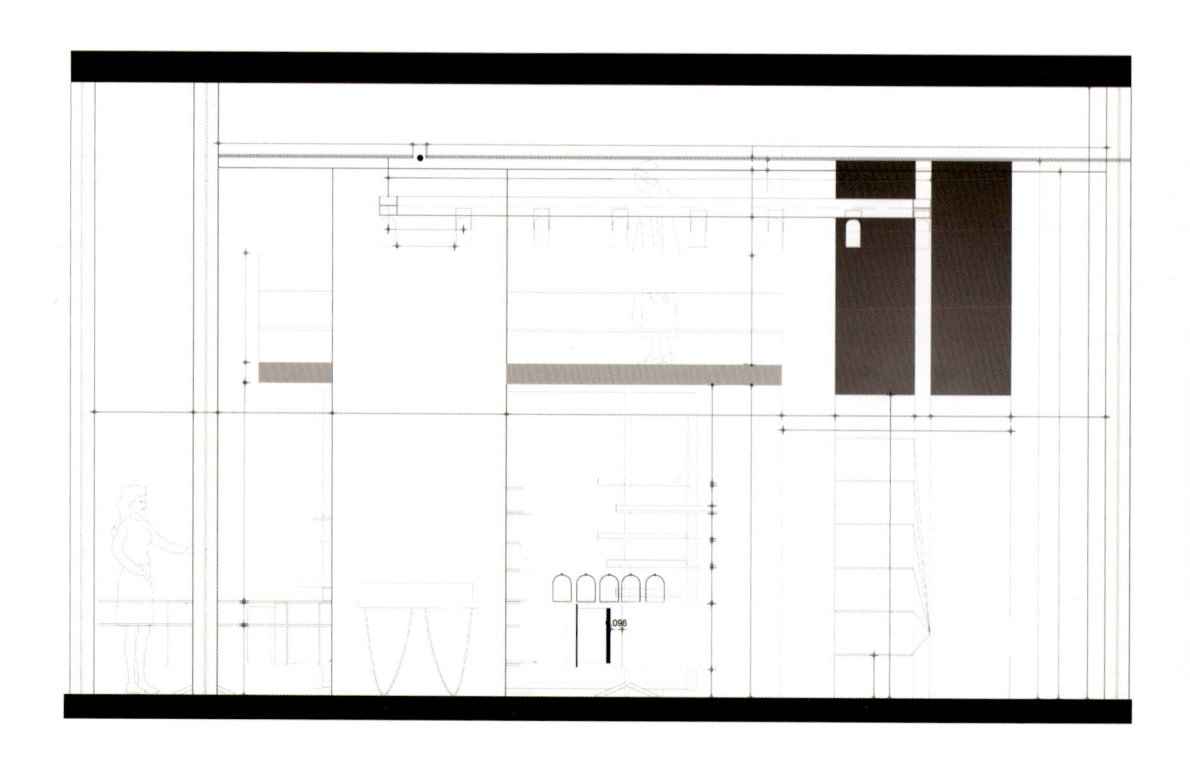

Section

7

6-7. The glass display counter
shining under the light
8-9. The unfinished wall and the
golden cage displaying products
contrasting each other

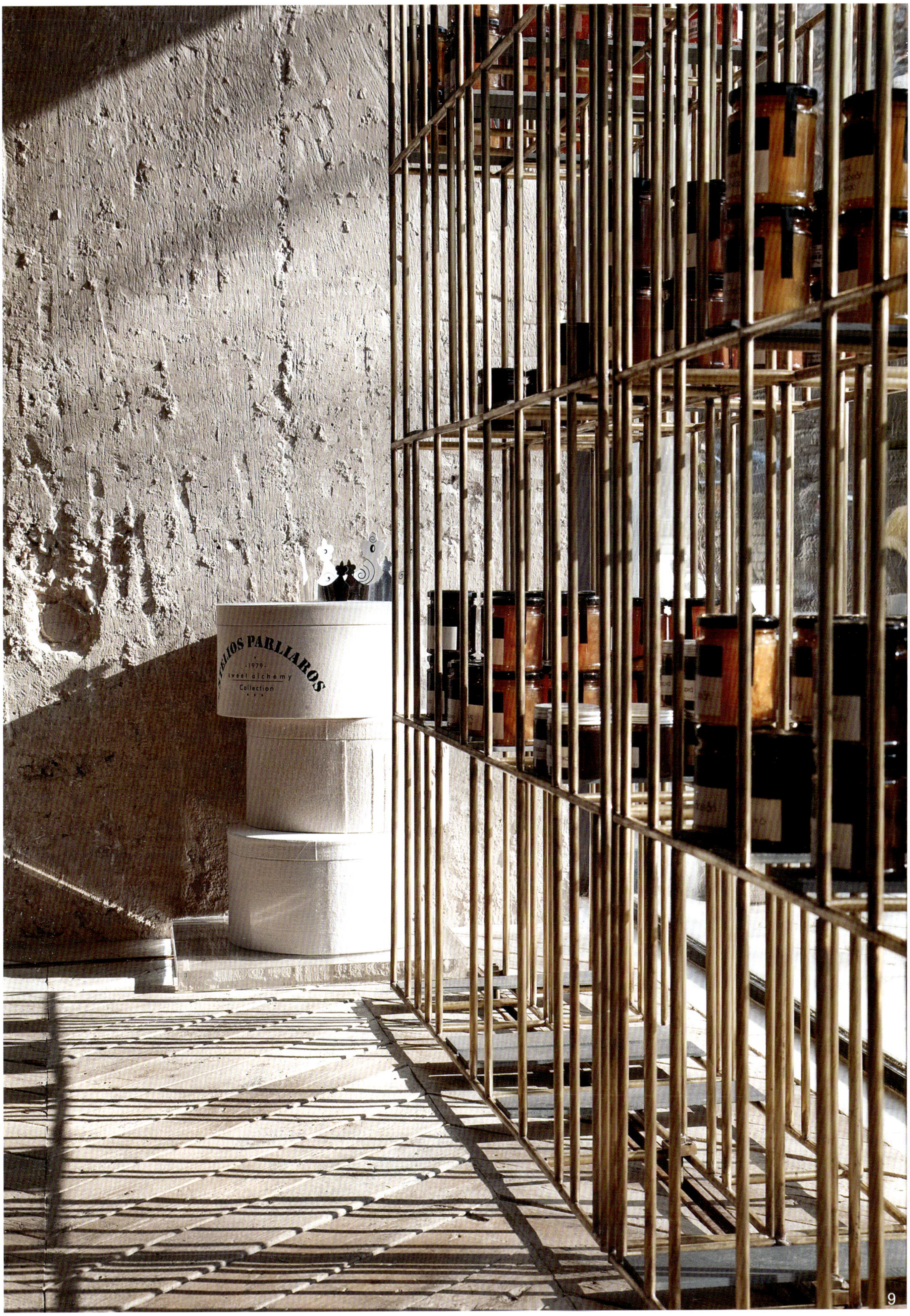

9

Chapter 3: *Holistic Design*

SUZUKAKE HONTEN

Designer: Koichi Futatsumata(CASE-REAL)
Location: Fukuoka, Japan
Project area: 163.2m²
Project year: 2008
Photographs: Hiroshi Mizusaki

'A Japanese pastry shop with Japanese black in silence' - a project of a Japanese pastry shop in Kami-Kawabata, Hakata Ward, Fukuoka City, a historical merchant town. A flagship shop of the Japanese pastry shop has Japanese 'Kaho', a pastry shop, and Japanese 'Saho', a tearoom. Under the idea that the place where pastries are treated is the holiest of holies, the 'Kaho', a pastry shop is independent from the crowd, even though the shop is on the main street. And to be conspicuous the existence of pure, simple pastries, there is only one half-floating, nine-metre display case in Japanese black. By using Japanese black plastered wall, the designer successfully abused the existence of the display case. In contrast to the 'Kaho', the designer made the 'Saho' to an open place with original produced furniture where everything inside can be easily recognised from the street. The entrance was made to be the symbolic existence of expectation for the previous state with a fascination decorated with a five-coloured curtain and a profound vermilion-lacquered signboard.

2

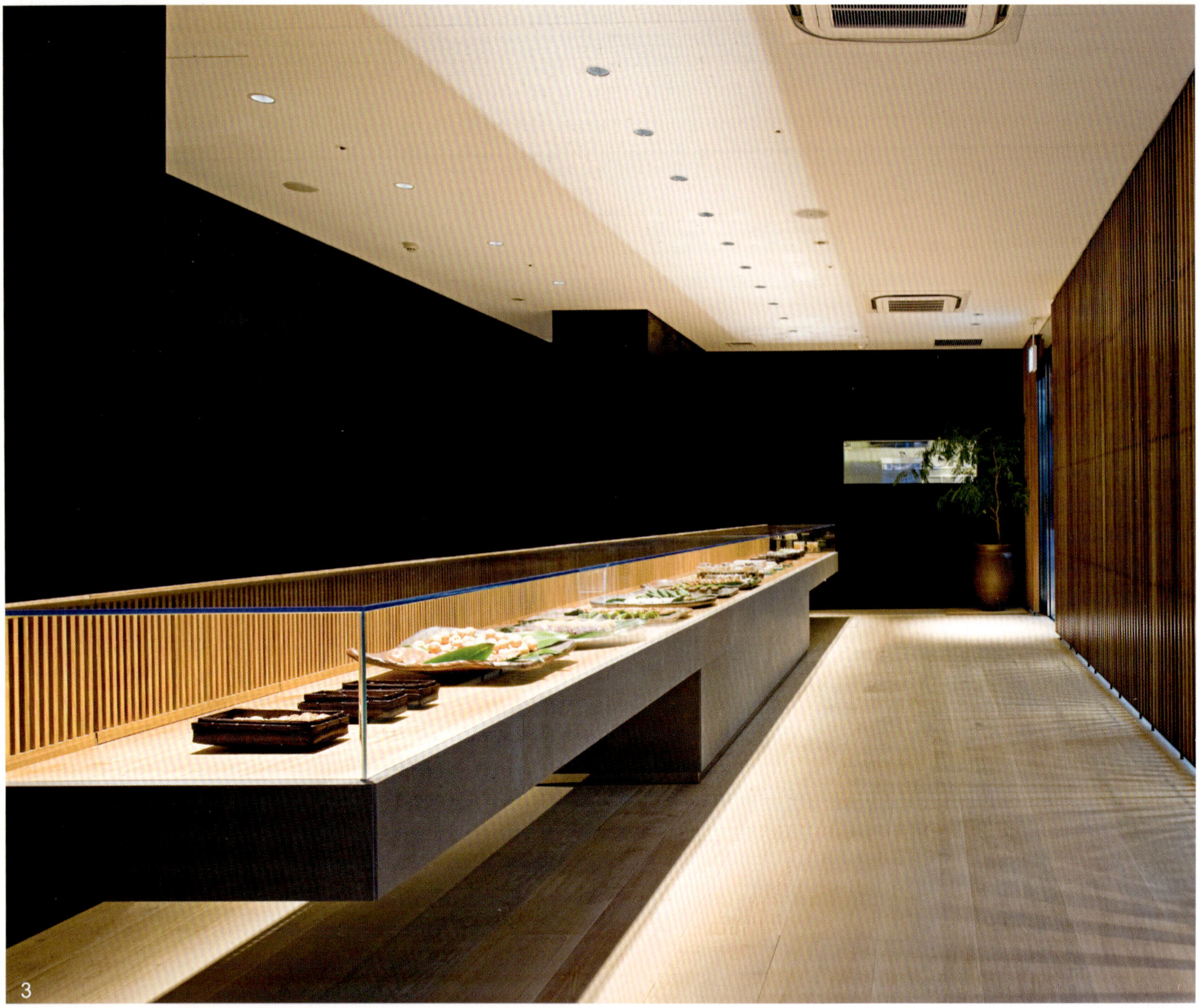
3

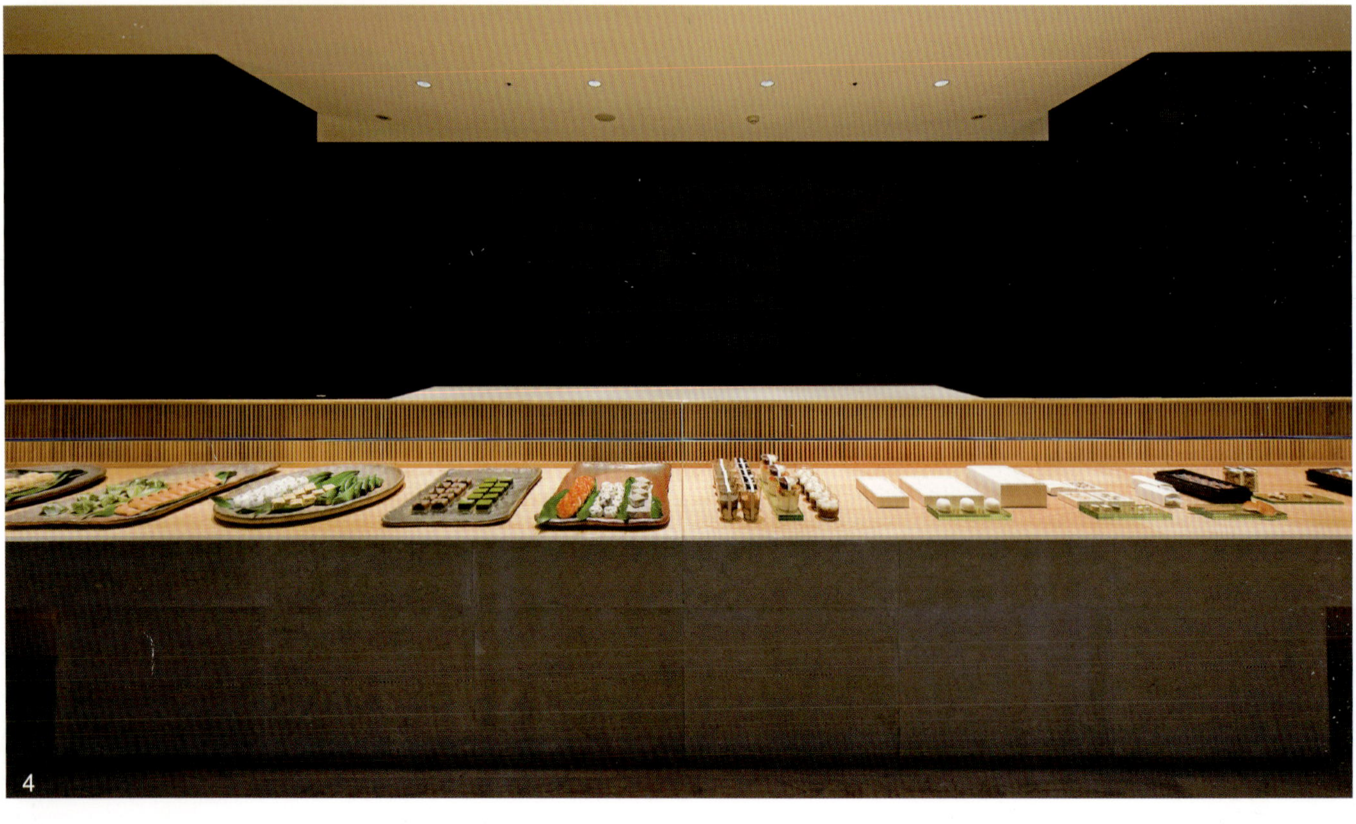
4

1. The display counter leaving shadows on the floor and adding playfulness to the space
2. The entrance with a five-coloured curtain and a profound vermilion-lacquered signboard being really eye-catching
3-4. The display counter is outstanding in the back ground of black wall, white ceiling and cream-coloured floor.
5. The entrance hall highlightig light colours and exuding natural feeling

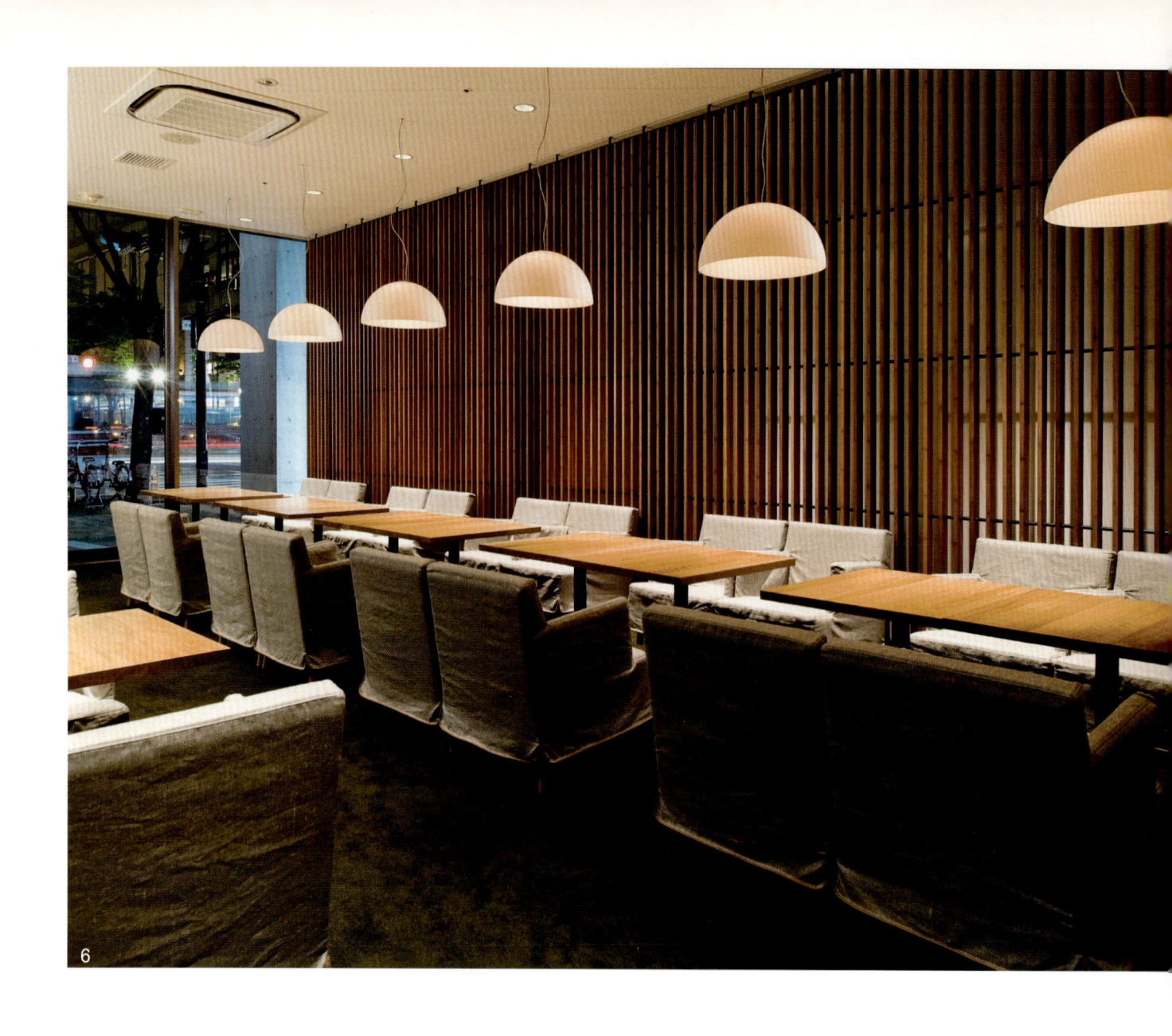

6-7. The tearoom emphasizing simple style

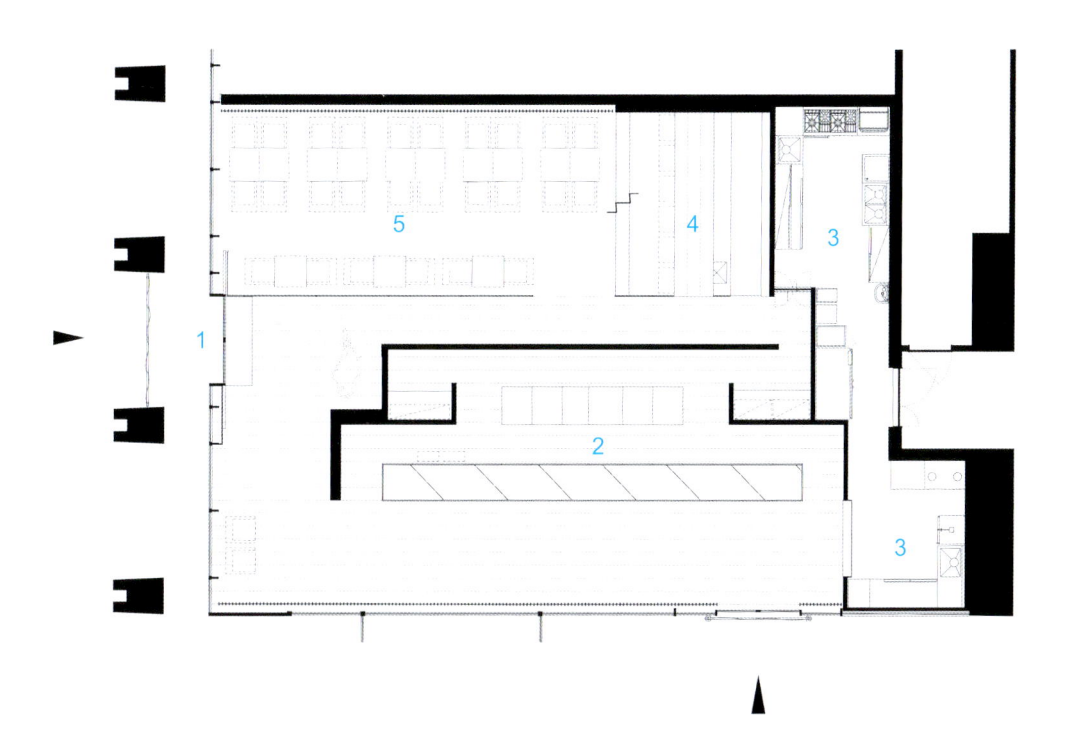

Floor Plan:
1. Entrance hall
2. Shop area
3. Kitchen
4. Counter
5. Tearoom

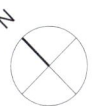

175

Chapter 3: Holistic Design

Little Cupcakes

Designer: Zwei Interiors Architecture
Location: Melbourne, Australia
Project year: 2011
Photographs: Michael Kai

Little Cupcakes was established in a little street of Melbourne in 2007 as one of the first cupcake bakeries in Melbourne CBD. Since 2007 Little cupcakes has been delivering freshly baked handmade cupcakes with passion and enthusiasm and now occupies three tenancies around the CBD.

Hidden within a Heritage Listed façade, the Queen Street Little Cupcakes shop/café celebrates the individuality and quirkiness of cupcakes. The beautiful façade is minimally treated with a monochrome colour palette and enlists a cupcake display in the window and subtle branding to entice customers.

Building on the existing Little Cupcakes brand, the client wanted to showcase their unique and delicious product range within an interior that reflects the personality of the brand. Recycled timber is used throughout, from the cupcake dis -play case to the banquette seating and wall-mounted shelving. Scattered cushions collected from local cottage industry screen printing houses create a soft, comfortable resting space for patrons.

In keeping with the heritage features of the tenancy, period style feature lighting drops over the small cafe tables and the servery maximising the sense of space and bringing the displayed cupcakes to life. The floor is tiled with a white mosaic and the existing stripped back ceiling painted out white, ensuring the eye is drawn to the quirky design features such as the Little Cupcakes wall decal, and most obviously, the vast offering of cupcakes.

177

Shopfront elevation

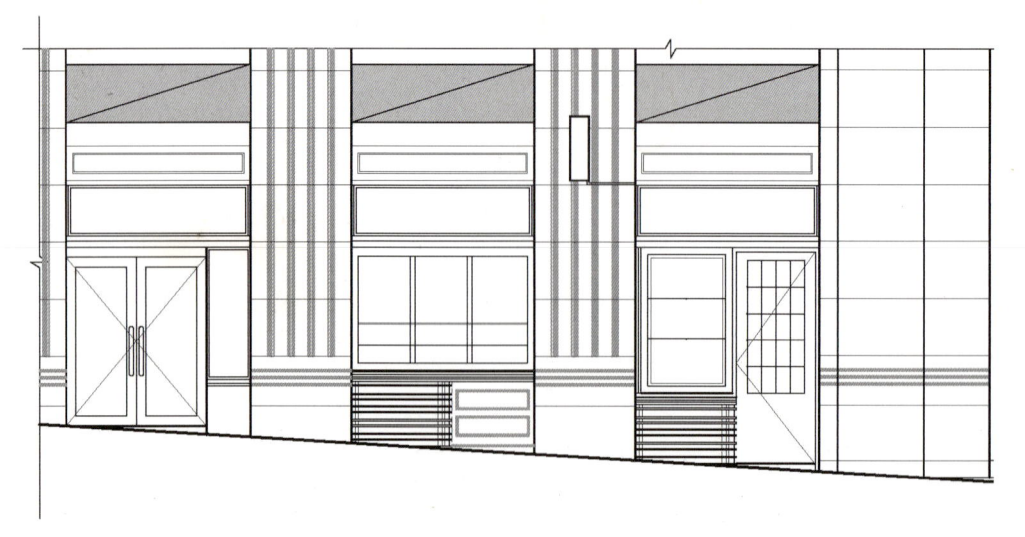

1-4. The shopfront showcasing simple style in monochrome colour palette and the use of large expanse of glass bringing the inside view out

5. The glass display cases completely showing the delicious cakes and the blackboard and wooden frame on the back wall adding interest to the space

6. The white mosaic floor and white floor, ceiling creating a simple background for furnitures and pastries

178

Coffee + mini cupcake
5 SENSES
(include Chai & Hot Choco)
$4.90
Exclude TEAS/ ICED DRINKS/ AFFOGATO.

6

7-8. Recycled timber is used in dining tables and chairs, and cushions are collected from local cottage industry screen printing houses, creating a warm homey atmosphere.

Handwritten annotations: natural wood / Clean display / Black Barrel & display / off white

SIMPLE CHAIRS
+ COAT RACK(DIY)

8

Floor Plan:
1. Entrance
2. Dining area
3. Display counter

181

Chapter 3: *Holistic Design*

Dynamic Café

Designer: Chrystalline Artchitect
Location: Jakarta, Indonesia
Project area: 56m²
Project year: 2009
Photographs: Soemario

The new Dynamic Café has successfully brought the ambiance of its space into a whole new level of coziness with the dominant use of rattans around the space.

Since the space is designated to function not only as a bakery, but as a café as well, the display and the seating area are both arranged with the interior of an open-spaced kitchen. This arrangement has been specifically created to deliver both attractive and interactive atmosphere to the viewers at the same time.

The surrounding walls are constructed with hazel patterned ceramics to accentuate the natural interior mood around the space. In addition to this, the floors are also polished with similar tiles to tone down any unnecessary flashing colours around, which lets the viewers' eyes to take in pleasure from the delicious pastry displayed and decorative rattans across the space.

The ceilings above were intended to be filled with a black out, which effectively helps to reduce the refracted light from the spot lighting and to put emphasis on the colour and surface appearances of the materials enclosing around the café.

Synthetic rattans are applied as the main materials to create decorative furniture and seats around the space. Meticulous details are also placed throughout the display island in the centre of it and around the hanging shelves with simple, light touches of metal, wood and rattans combined together. Moreover, every colour, patterns and textures poured into the room are all pure; natural colours of the materials re-highlight the warm nature of the space. As a result, these combinations along with the fresh pastries displayed have diminished the frigidity aura, and are replaced with flourishing natural homelike feeling towards the viewers.

As for the lighting itself, halogen spot lightings and fancy, ornamental hanging lamps are placed which effectively give off hints of spontaneity into the space and break off the monotonous pattern. And though the lamps are shaped with a more dynamic and striking pattern, the natural material has complement the lights with its surroundings, blending them to create a radiating homely atmosphere around the space.

Dynamic cafe

184

1. The main tones of the space in harmonious with the colours of the logo
2-4. The display cases being different in material and form
5. The dining area in the centre of the space and seeking harmony with the surrounding
6-7. Ornamental hanging lamps breaking off the monotonous pattern
8-9. Wood tables and rattan chairs combined together to create a natural and warm atmosphere

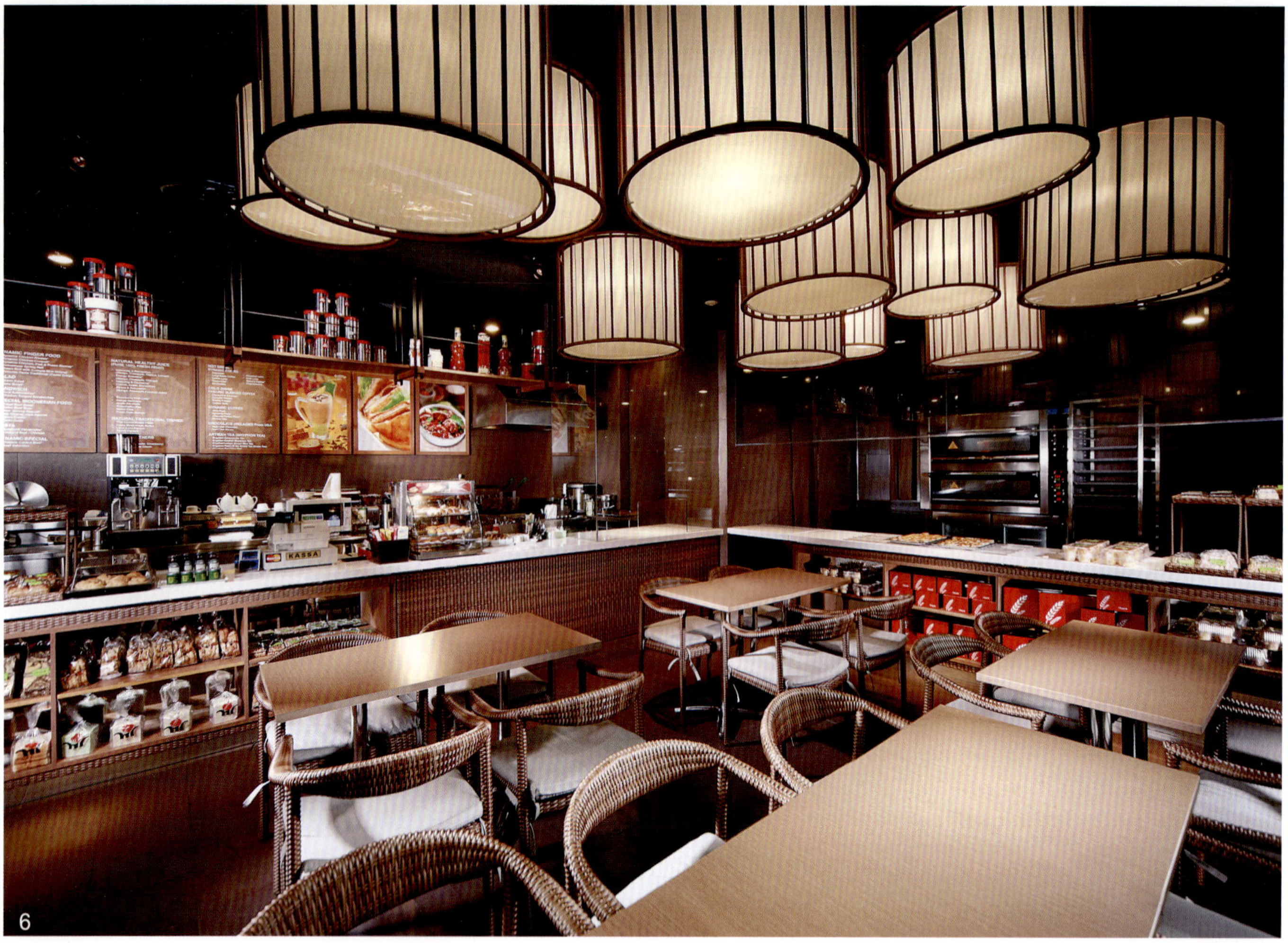

6

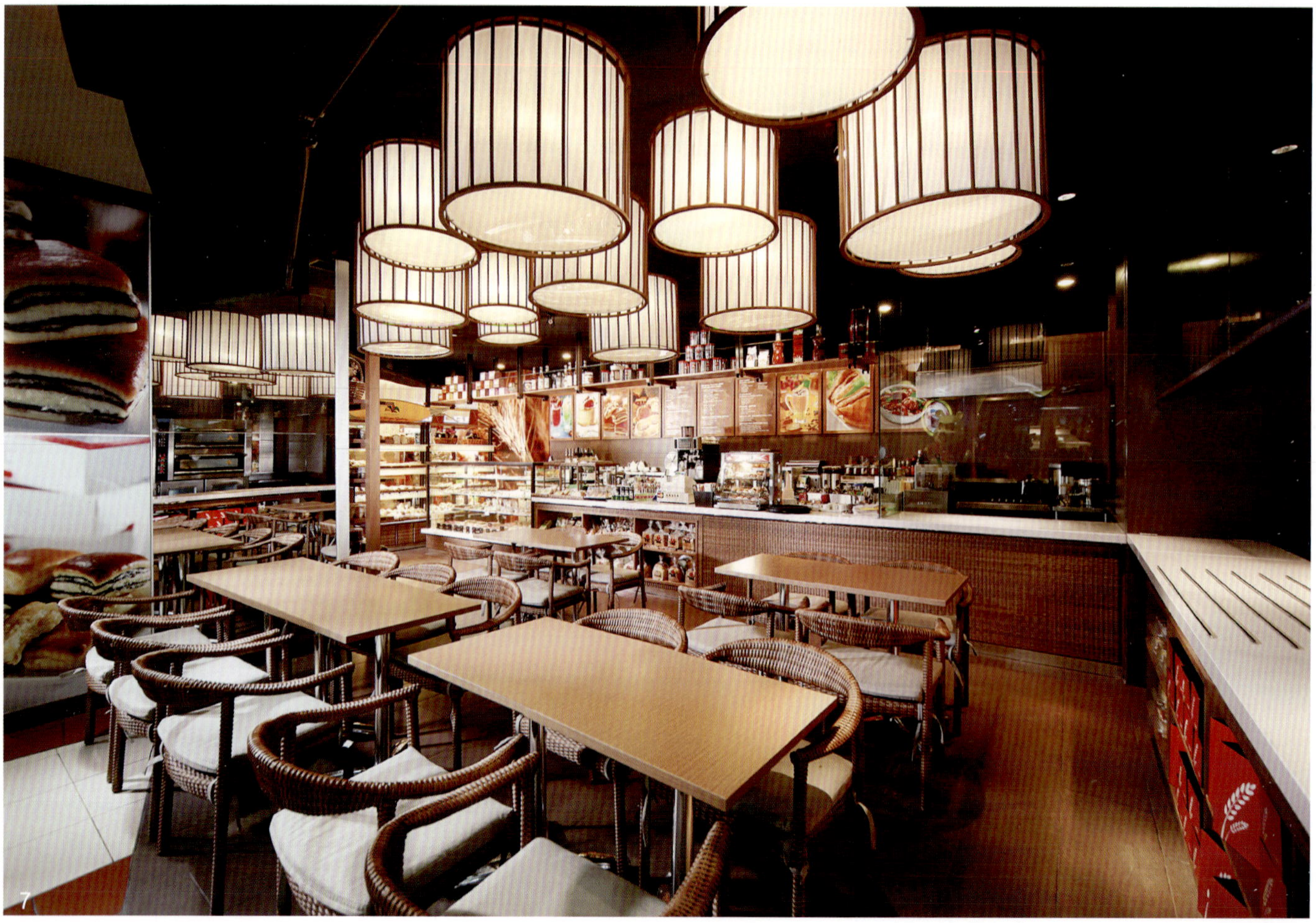
7

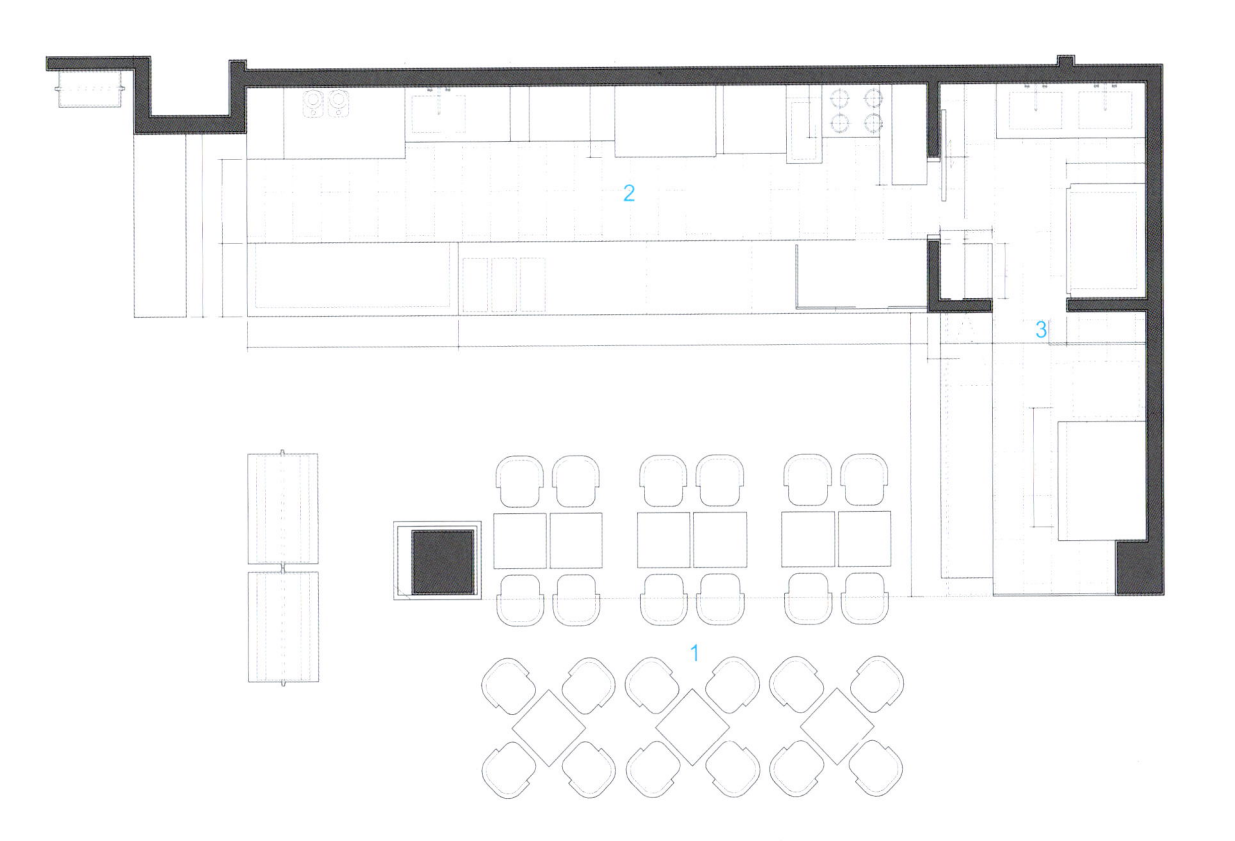

Floor Plan:
1. Seating area
2. Kitchen area
3. Dishes area

187

Chapter 3: Holistic Design

4. Economical Ways to Update Existing Bakery

If an existing bakery looks a bit old and stale, some interior design changes should be considered. There are several ways to update and refresh the operation without having to do a complete renovation.

Freshen Up with Paint
Nothing brightens or freshens up a room better than a new coat of paint. Painting is the easiest and most inexpensive way to make an instant change to the interior design of the existing operation. It's also a good excuse for the owner to clean and freshen up the walls. Choose a colour that works well with the brand, but is still trendy and modern. Don't just stick to the walls. Repaint the chairs, counters, tables – anything that is looking a bit old, dirty or faded.

[Handwritten note: Warm Colour, different colour for Chair]

Hang Wallpaper
If the owner wants wood walls in the bakery, but can't afford it for economic reason, then wallpaper that looks like wood can be selected. The variety of wallpaper available today makes it possible to achieve practically any look one wants for a fraction of the price. Consider using wallpaper with different textures to add to the visual depth of the operation.

Use Mirrors
Mirrors are a great way to create extra light, space and accents. Framed mirrors can create mock windows as well. Place mirrors around the bakery counter to multiply the images of the fresh breads, cookies, cakes and pastries, and make things appear more plentiful.

[Handwritten note: rear glass of display unit]

Paint the Floors
If new flooring is needed, but can't afford hardwood, consider removing the existing flooring (whether it's carpet, laminate or tile) to expose the concrete, then painting it. The operator can be creative with the colours, patterns and designs. The brand logo even can be painted on the floor. Alternatively, lots of inexpensive laminate tiles that look like hardwood but cost a lot less can be found and selected.

Get New Fabric
Instead of buying new chairs and banquettes, consider reupholstering the existing furniture. Look for fabrics that are durable and easy to clean. Fabric stores often have blowout sales on last year's styles. If the operator wants the bakery to be more eclectic, consider using fabric from the scrap bin. Many designer fabric stores have remnants that one can buy to use on chairs, lampshades, or anything else that needs a little sprucing up. If the operator has dining chairs with only the seats upholstered, the job can be done on one's own – just pop the seat out, stretch the new fabric over the seat and staple it into place.

Look for Second-hand options
Scour garage sales and flea markets, restaurant auctions, or websites like eBay, Craigslist and Kijiji to find stuff for cheap. Buying second-hand products is essential to interior designing on a budget. Look for detail pieces and think outside the box. For example, you could use an old iron gate as a storage rack for pots or an old ladder (with a fresh coat of paint) as a stand.

[handwritten: → use old furniture]

Be Creative with Props *[handwritten: & dress up]*
Dress up the bakery by picking up glass vases at the dollar store, and filling the jars with stones, marbles, rocks or sand, and a candle. The operator can also create visual merchandising displays by using items found in the kitchen such as glass jars, tins, boxes, old baking equipment and utensils.

[handwritten: old baking tins & equipment utensils]

Work with Artists on Consignment
There are a lot of starving artists out there today who would love the opportunity to display their artwork to the public. Work on consignment with the artist whereby the operator agrees to hang the artwork in the bakery, and if a piece is sold, the operator can get to keep a percentage of the sales. This is a win-win situation: the operator get original artwork to improve the interior design of the space while the artist gets the opportunity to gain some exposure.

[handwritten: Artwork]

A little creativity will go a long way in helping the bakery put its best face forward.

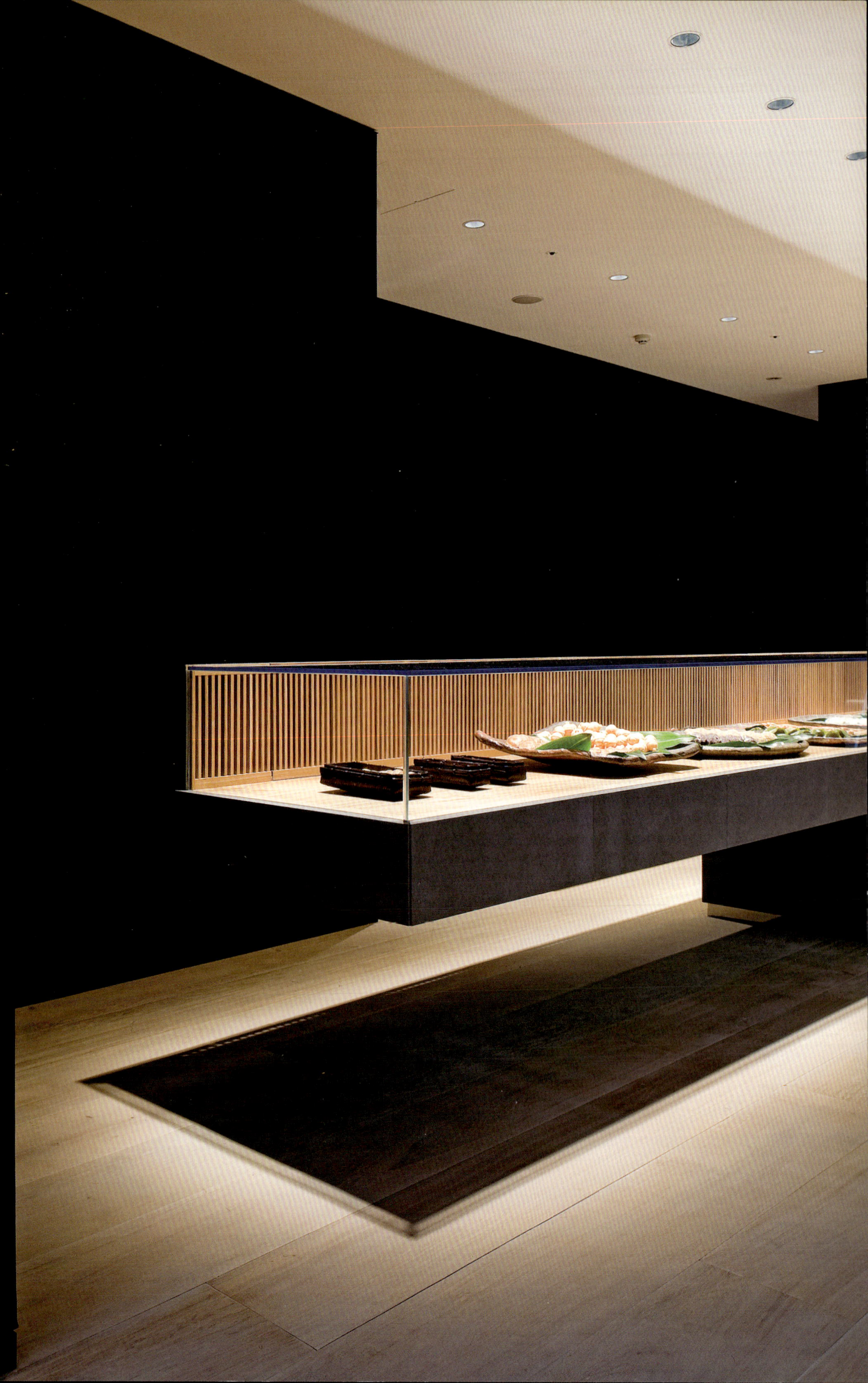

Chapter 4: Display

1. Client's Demands

2. Display Case

3. Tips to Improve Displays

Chapter 4: Display

Creating a good display is integral to increasing the bakery's business and ensuring its success. To achieve this, a number of factors that contribute to the creation of an appealing display should be considered.

1. Client's Demands

A key concern expressed by bakery shop clients involves maximizing stock turnover. The highly perishable nature of bakery products means that they must be sold shortly after manufacture to ensure that freshness and quality is maintained. This means that product display impact, and product quantity, must be optimized within the store design.

2. Display Case

Bakery display cases often perform a significant role in showcasing the look as well as protecting the quality of these delightful and also attractive treats. It is rather essential to maintain the cooked items inside the bakery display case and safeguard all of them until it's time to serve.

Refrigeration
If the pastries have to be chilled, the refrigeration system is required within the display case in order to keep all of them cool and stop icing from melting. Cakes, slices and desserts will often require consistent refrigeration within their displays and condensation must be prevented as it causes the goods to spoil as well as impairing visibility of the display.

Lighting
Recent surveys conducted on bakery customers reveal that product appearance is the most important factor for customers to make an impulse purchase. Aroma came in second, followed by price, and customer service.

Baked goods are visually enticing so prominent displays with lighting that flatters the colour of the product, support high turnover. A customer is often enticed to stop and make a purchase from the bakery by the rich and vibrant colours of the diversified cakes, pastries, and yummy treats that line the display case. Without the proper lighting in the bakery department, the freshness and appeal to the customer is lost and so is the sale.

The significance of using a very well lighted display case can help the consumer observe every detail of the freshly baked sweets. Numerous bakery display cases include top lighting which can sparkle straight down on the display racks; nevertheless, certain cases are not designed with this particular essential feature and rely on ambient light to filter to the lower pastries. It always pays off to have shelf lights under each shelf so that all of the pastries can be seen. If cakes are set onto tiered shelves within a display fridge it is recommended to provide even lighting under each shelf so none of the product sits in the shadow of those above, unsold at end of day.

Air Circulation + fan

Baked goods also require efficient air circulation if they are to be displayed whilst still warm, and having these on open display can also assist in having scent play a compelling part in attracting the consumer. There are very few people who do not find the scent of freshly baked breads and cakes extremely enticing. Bake small batches of goods throughout the day to attract customers with aroma. If possible, use a fan to blow the bakery smells out onto the street to entice passers-by. An inviting aroma is a great in-store bakery sales driver!

Chapter 4: Display

Deli House Bakery

Designer: edha architects
Location: North Jakarta, Indonesia
Project area: 80m²
Project year: 2010
Photographs: Fernando Gomulya (Techtography)

Aisian Style

Deli House Bakery as one of the bakeries in the midst of the shopping centre, wants to emphasise in simple, clean, innovative but still elegant characteristic. With that approach as the base, illustration of how 'bread' is made, described by a space which dominated with white and brown coloured curves, using materials that give a warm image.

The display area and cashier are placed in the front area of the shop, while the back area are functioned as kitchen and storage room. In the middle of the shop, the main display area appears as two solid and massive display elliptical tables, with white duco paint as the finishing, and two levels of tempered glass on the top, supported by a stainless structure both vertically and horizontally. And for the lighting, there are thin elliptical solid forms with warm white coloured cove lighting in it which were hanged on the stainless structure of the ceiling.

The walls of the store functioned as additional display area and storage for some goods. On the surface of the wall, there are several 'curved tear' forms which are functioned as the additional display. Exception for the middle area wall, the 'curved tear' is functioned as a 'visual' point, where customers can watch how the bread was made by the pâtissière at the kitchen. The additional display is made as pits on the wall, to give a 'floating' effect to the two levels tempered glass on the top of the main display table. Mirrors are used as the background of it (the pits on the wall), and black mirrors for the artificial 'curved tear'. Those additional displays got white coloured duco paint for the outer surface as the finishing, giving a connected feeling to the wall, while for the inner surface finished by dark brown coloured duco paint.

Consistently, the 'curved tears' also appear on the ceiling finished by brown coloured duco paint, along with the cove lighting as part of it. Those appearances of the 'curved tears' on the ceiling fused with the ones on the wall. The cashier table appears as a solid form, just like the bottom part of the main display table, with the same finishing too, and accompanied by the L-formation warm white coloured down light lamps as the lighting. For the floor finishing, parquet is chosen to create a warmer image to the whole store area. The façade of the store is created by following the form of half bread. And it can be seen as a whole bread when it's fused with the reflection of itself on the floor.

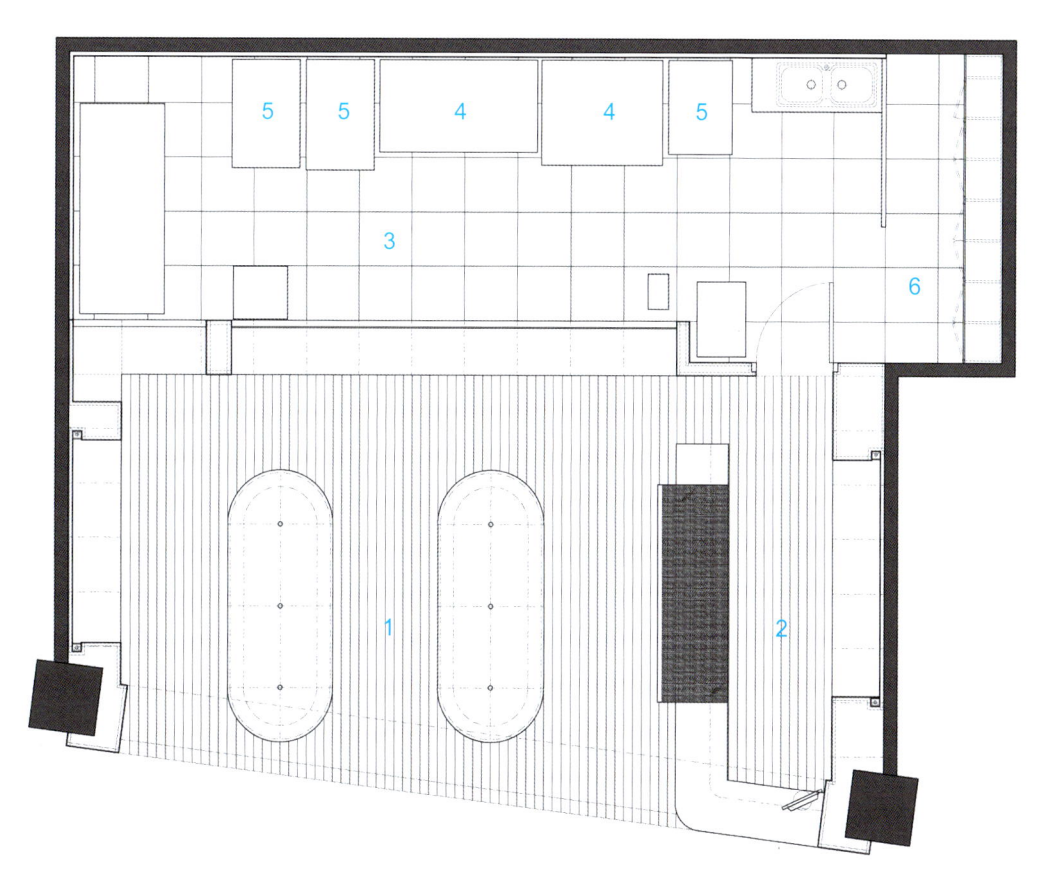

Floor Plan:
1. Display area
2. Cashier area
3. Kitchen area
4. Oven
5. Proofer
6. Locker area

195

1. The façade of the store takes the form of half bread and can seen as a whole bread when fused with the reflection of itself on the floor.
2. The main display area of two solid and massive display elliptical tables with white duco paint as the finishing, and two levels of tempered glass on the top, supported by a stainless structure both vertically and horizontally.
3. The cashier counter performing the function of displaying as well

197

Deli House
WONDERFULL LIFE
Rp.15.000,-
Deli House
OCEAN PARK
Deli House
LOVELY
Deli House
DENMARK PEACH

4

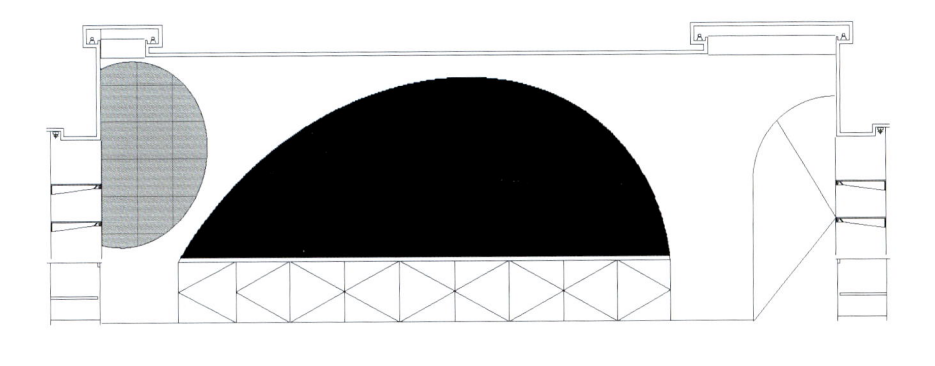

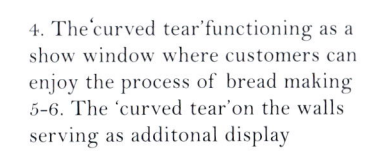

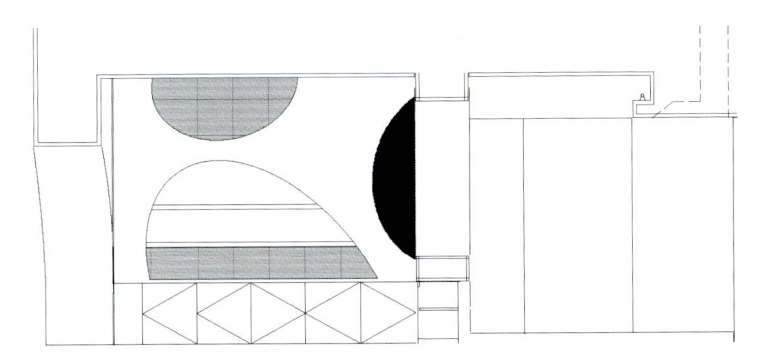

4. The 'curved tear' functioning as a show window where customers can enjoy the process of bread making
5-6. The 'curved tear' on the walls serving as additonal display

Sections

199

Chapter 4: Display

Dynamic Grand Indonesia

Designer: Chrystalline Architect
Location: Jakarta, Indonesia
Project area: 81m²
Project year: 2010
Photographs: William Sebastian

The new Dynamic bakery was created with a strong, modern, thematic design. It is a compelled mixture of traditional, warm values combined with natural, contemporary traits together, creating a homely, and yet dynamic design for the pleasure of the viewers' eyes.

The space mainly uses materials which were either pastel coloured or naturally the colour of the material itself. Hence, this colour scheme creates a room with a very natural and relaxing state of ambience. Some hints of steel beams were placed around the room to give a bit of sophisticated and dynamic feature into the space.

One of the most unique attributes in this construction is the existence of carts and green wall on the side of the bakery. The carts are built based on the traditional carts from Indonesia to deliver the traditional and homely sense of feelings toward the viewers. The pastries then were served in a synthetic rattan basket with an inclined angle to give easier access for the viewers to look at the pastries displayed.

To accentuate an even more natural feel, the walls behind the carts were transformed into green walls with decorative leaves to create touches of natural scenery to the atmosphere of the space.

The island counters were constructed also to suit the ambience within the rooms. The counters were built into four levels, with the descending size from the base to the top. The synthetic rattans are used as its main material as the base counter, with some shaped into baskets placed on every level of wood plank. These ripples within the baskets are created to give off light texture to the design. Each level was based with wood planks for stronger foundation. Beneath the wood plank, continuous lights were placed. Covered with white, soft fabrics to reduce the intensity from the spotlights, but still enough light to radiate around the pastries displayed.

The ceilings are designed to be in a black out with halogen lights placed along the ceilings, which give off a more striking and appealing lighting effect, catching the eyes of the viewers. The meticulous decorations placed around the counters give an accent for the viewers' eyes to indulge.

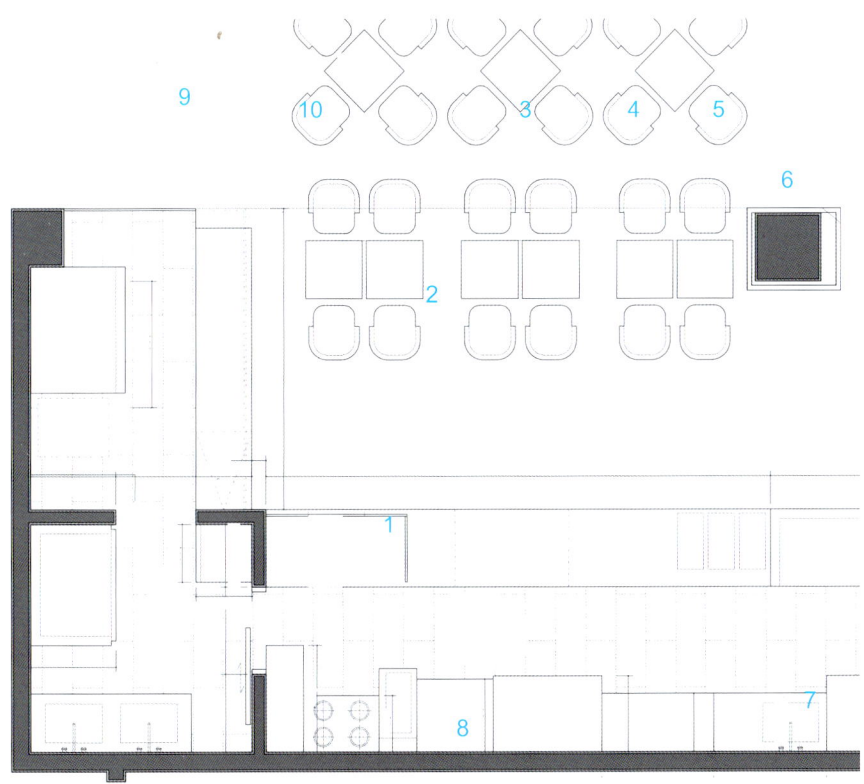

Floor Plan:
1. Bread display
2. Cashier
3. Freezer
4. Chiller oven
5. Moveable oven tray
6. Showcase
7. Special display
8. Display area
9. Wastafel
10. Under counter chiller

201

1. The entire space exuding homely and warm atmosphere
2-3. The island counters built into four levels, with the descending size from the base to the top and the synthetic rattans used as its main material as the base counter, with some shaped into baskets placed on every level of wood

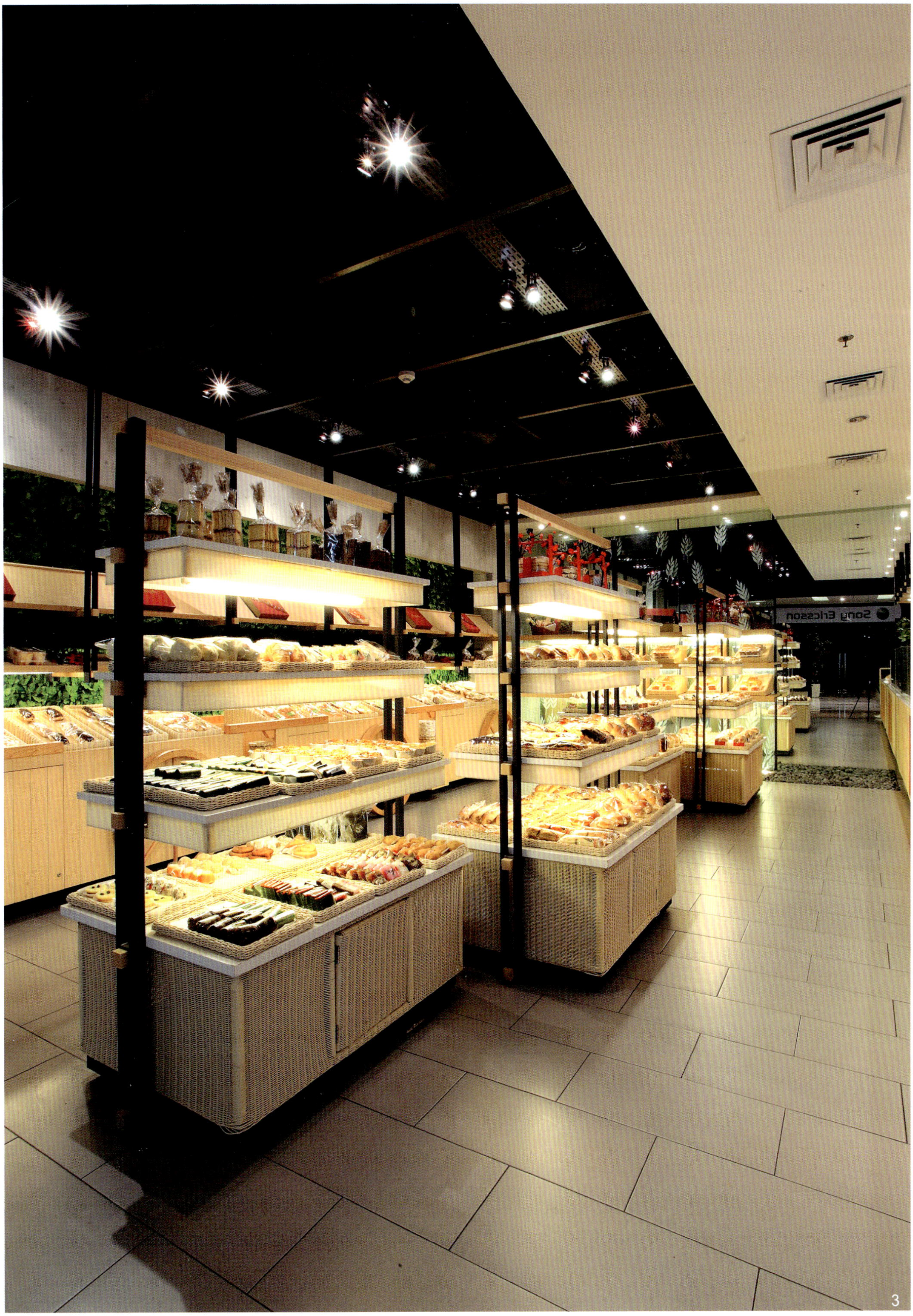

3

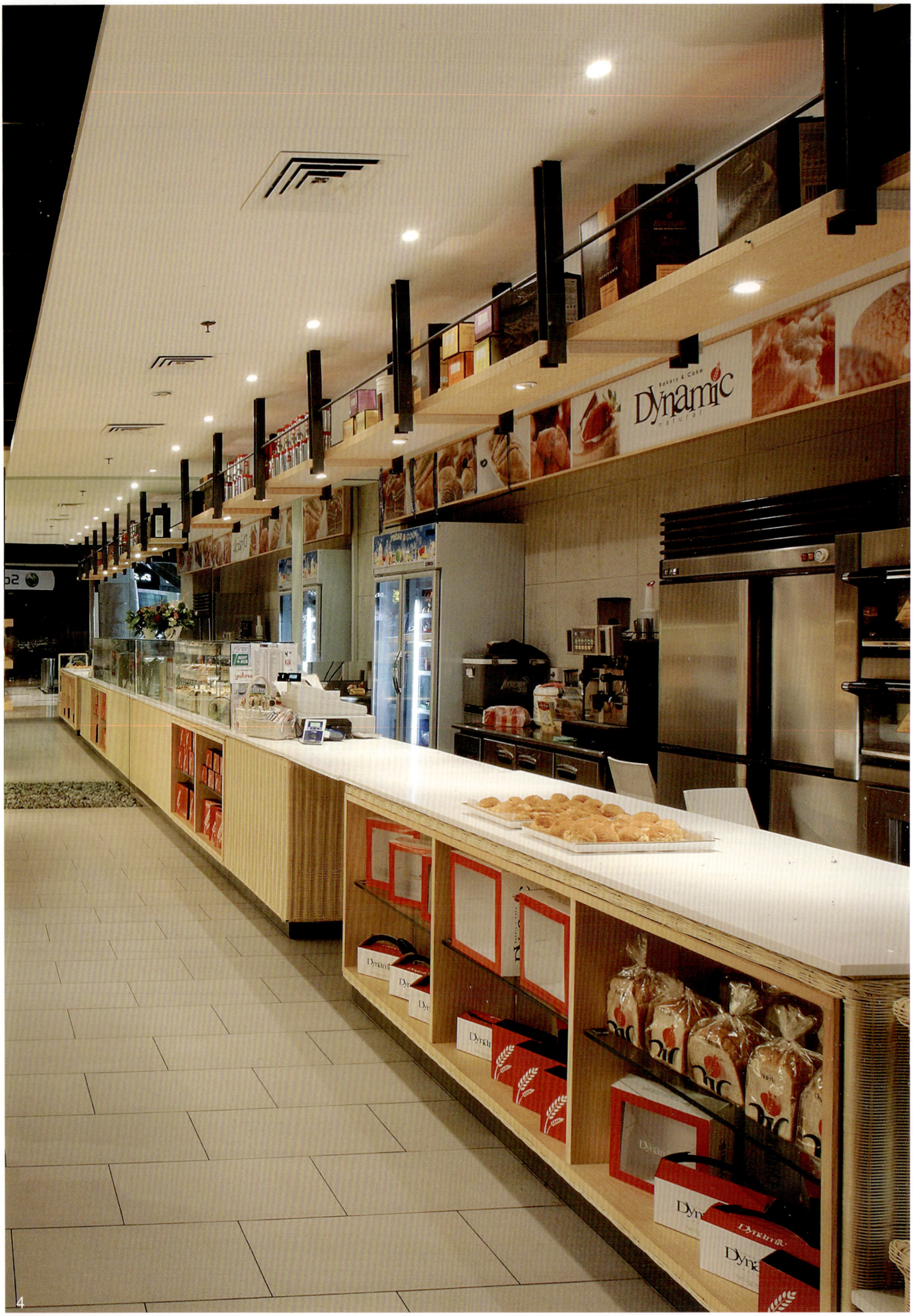

4

1 overhead display storage
2 rear

4. Display counter along the preparation area
5-6. The carts and green wall on the side of the bakery as the unique feature of the store and highlighting the Indonesia style and the pastries then served in a synthetic rattan basket with an inclined angle to give easier access for the viewers to look at the pastries displayed

Chapter 4: *Display*

La Maison du Macaron

Designer: Mario Painchaud/c3studio
Location: Montreal, Canada
Project area: 30m²
Project year: 2010
Photographs: Steve Montpetit

Two main challenges arose while developing the gourmet bakery, La Maison du Macaron in Montreal: the cramped and narrow premises (3metres × 10 metres) and the distinct features of the products that needed to be displayed.

The predominance of white in the design gives the boutique its general appearance, the only exception being the burgundy porcelain floor that extends onto the partially lit back wall, covering it subtly with decorative patterns.

A high white carrera marble counter, covered with a tempered glass case, crosses the room from one end to the other, contributing to defining the space. More than 700 coloured macaroons are highlighted and reflected on the ceiling made with white stretched vinyl. Inescapably, the ceiling is a strong element that enhances the client experience and acts as an important element in the general marketing approach. Well lit built-in alcoves create additional display space and add a whole other dimension to the space. Opalescent, milky-white neutral lighting gives the space just the right rhythm and creates a perfect ambiance for products displayed.

Reflection is essential in this project: marble, glass, vinyl, shiny laminate and the use of only one piece of furniture that unfolds to imitate a ribbon, create depth and contribute to di-minishing the physical limits of space.

The result is impressive as clients enter into a simple space, yet one which reveals a strong, remarkable identity, inviting customers to indulge in their pastries.

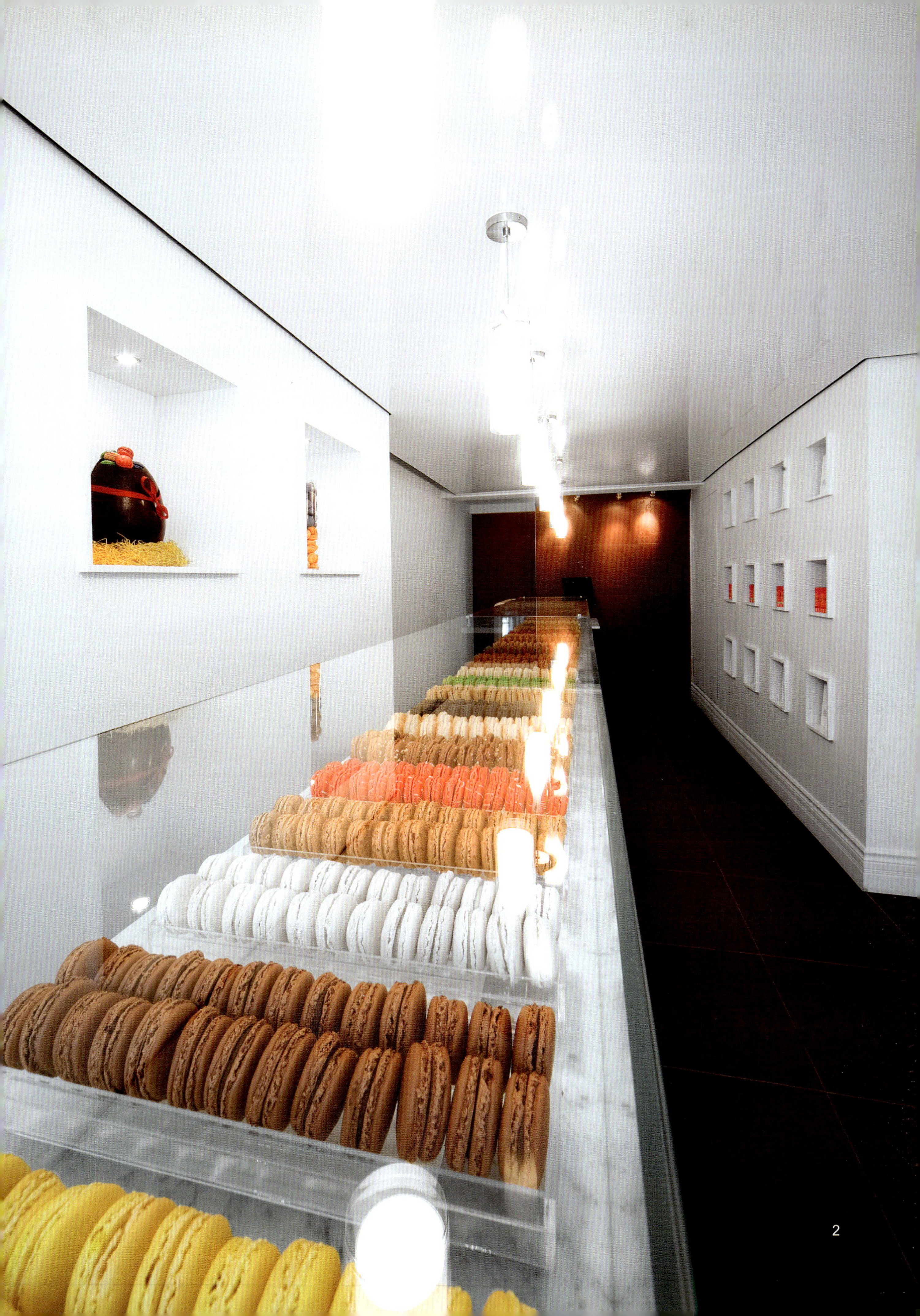

2

1. Colourful cakes functioning as ornaments of the shop
2. The high white carrera marble counter, covered with a tempered glass case, extending from one end to the other to define the space
3-4. Well lit built-in alcoves creating additional display space and opalescent, milky-white neutral lighting giving the space just the right rhythm and contributing a perfect ambiance for products displayed
5. The burgundy porcelain floor extending onto the partially lit back wall serving as the only exception of the white tone

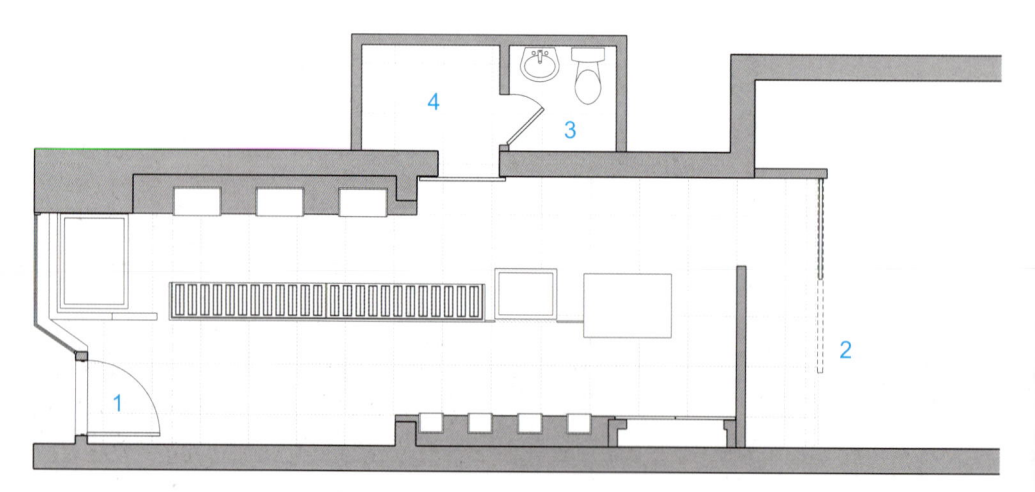

Color – white & dark brick red.

Floor Plan:
1. Store
2. Kitchen
3. Bathroom
4. Storage

208

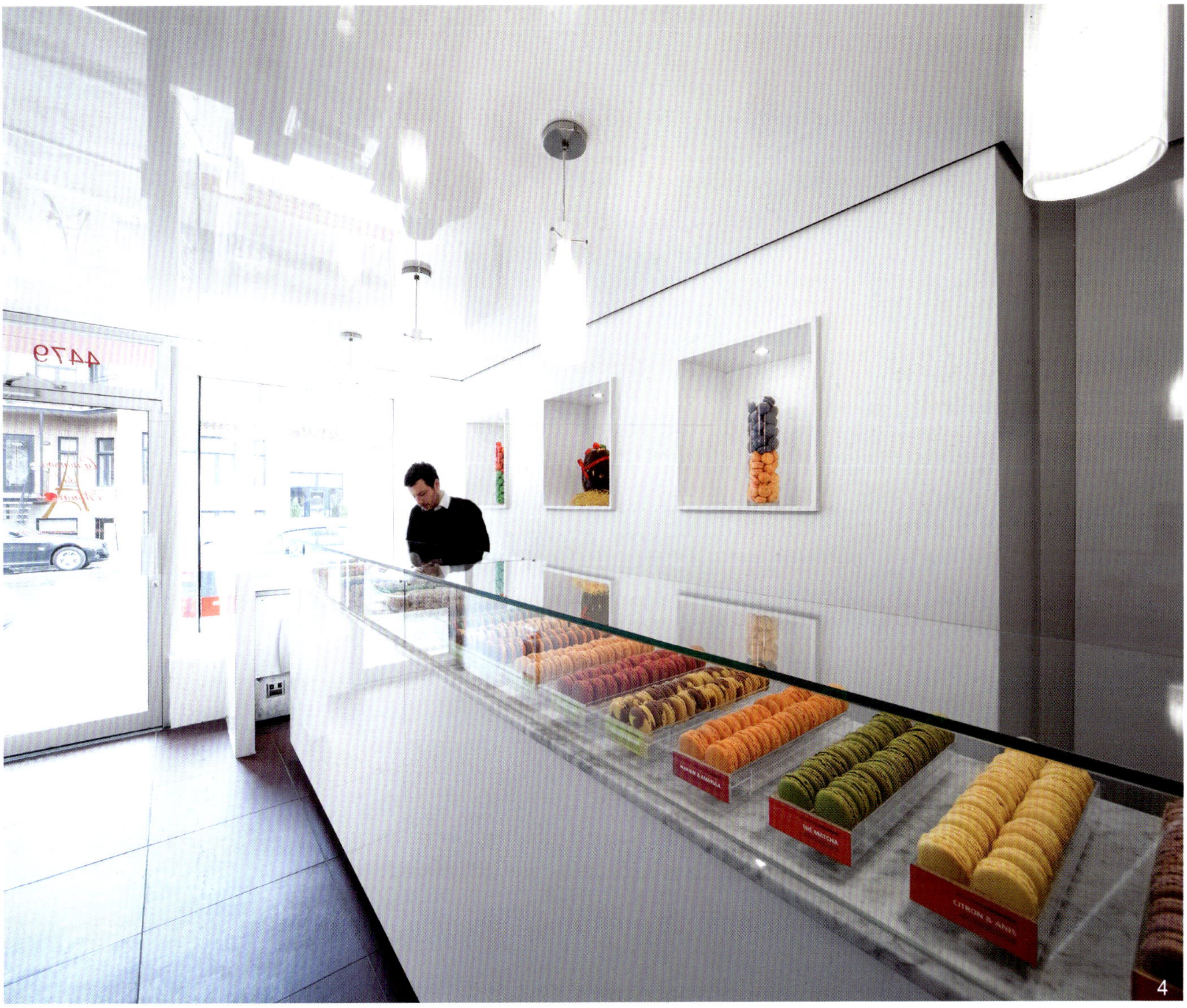

4

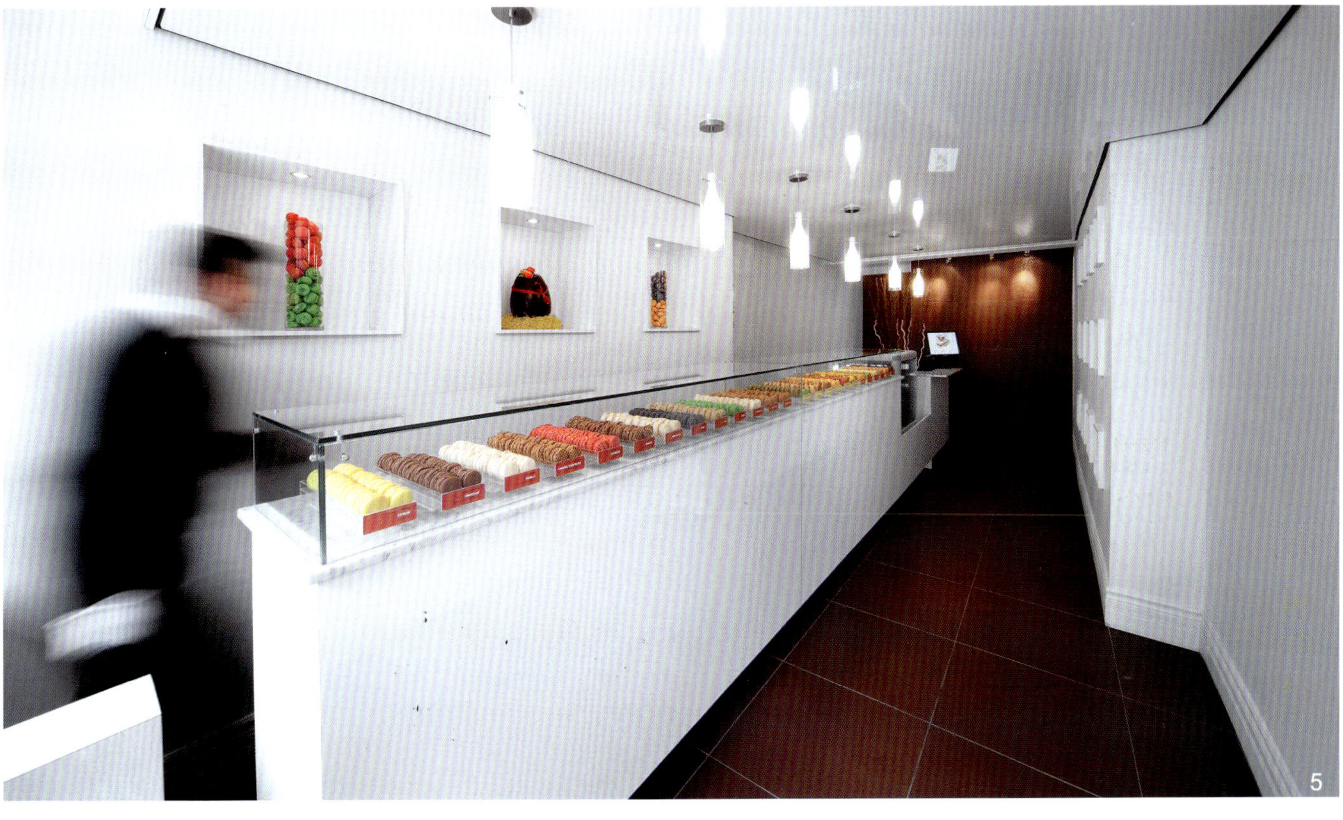
5

6. Branches used as adornments adding interest to the space
7. Cakes on display being seen from outside

MACARONS · MACARONS GLACÉS · DESSERTS AUX FRUITS FRAIS
PIÈCES ARTISTIQUES DE MACARONS · MARIAGES ET

7

Chapter 4: Display

3. Tips to Improve Displays

The first rule of thumb for displaying baked goods is to treat every item with the utmost care. Do not pile, stack or cram the products onto a shelf. Not only is this visually unappealing, but it is most likely damaging the products as well.

To determine where a certain bakery may be missing out on opportunities for selling freshly baked products, take a look at what customers see when they enter the bakery. Shoppers tend to stay to their right-hand side when they first walk into a bakery, and continue walking along the perimeter to do much of their buying. Thus, the owner should bring the fresh products right up front to the customer, and make sure these products are of the highest quality, well presented and delivered with excellent customer service. They can also position the breads on a tiered table placed right at the entrance of the bakery. Next to the table, offer customers free samples of hot bread fresh from the oven with a variety of jams, butters and spreads that also sell. (Figure 1-5)

(1)The product displays must also fit to the trays, plates or baskets in which the baked goods and cakes will be displayed and if the product is fragile, the designer must ensure that the client's staff can easily lift out and pack the cake for the customer.

(2)Keep specialty breads separate from traditional breads to draw attention to their uniqueness. Use proper signage to indicate what makes these breads so special, such as the ingredients used or the unique way that made them.

(3)Use traditional baking equipments such as flour bags and scoops, wooden breadboards and shelves, wicker baskets and pottery to add authenticity to displays.

(4)Desserts are largely regarded as an impulse buy in most bakeries. They are best sold at or near the cash register, on top of the bakery counter, on the top row of a display case or at the take-out pickup point. Another great place to sell dessert items is to place them wherever customers wait to be served. As they wait, they look around. And who can resist buying a tempting dessert treat?

(5)People also tend to purchase desserts based on size. The bigger the better. They are also always looking for something unusual, especially when it comes to shape. Thus, desserts of big size and unusual shape are better displayed at conspicuous place.

(6)If display cases are employed, highlight and dress up products by pairing them with fresh fruits, herbs, flowers or even a bottle of champagne. All those props help to convey the feeling of freshness.

(7)Offer free samples aside the new products displayed! One cannot stress how beneficial sampling can be for bakeries. Giving customers a chance to taste products and opportunities to ask questions is the best way to realise a sale. Sampling also gives staff an opportunity to educate customers. It is probably the best merchandising tool a bakery has available.

(8)Seasonal displays, appealing product presentation, product bundling,- can drive impulse and repeat sales.

Figure 1-5. Various displaying patterns being helpful to promote the products and at the same time enticing customers to buy

215

σουμάδα
υφάλμυρα καραμελωμένα αμύγδαλα
υφάλμυρα ζαχαρωμένα αμύγδαλα
υφάλμυρα καραμελωμένα αμύγδαλα
υφάλμυρα ζαχαρωμένα αμύγδαλα
υφάλμυρα καραμελωμένα αμύγδαλα
υφάλμυρα ζαχαρωμένα αμύγδαλα
ΤΖΙΝΤΖΕΡ
ΤΖΙΝΤΖΕΡ
ΤΖΙΝΤΖΕΡ
υφάλμυρα ζαχαρωμένα αμύγδαλα
sweet alchemy
υφάλμυρα ζαχαρωμένα αμύγδαλα
ΛΕΜΟΝΙ ΓΛΑΣΣΕ
ΛΕΜΟΝΙ ΓΛΑΣΣΕ
ΛΕΜΟΝΙ ΓΛΑΣΣΕ
ALMOND
sweet alchemy
σουμάδα

Chapter 5: Design Guidelines and Standards

1. Premises, Equipment and Vehicles

2. Furniture, Utensils and Floor

3. Cleanliness and Sanitation

4. Sitting or Lounging Equipment

5. Lighting and Safety Lighting

6. Wearing Apparel

7. Keeping and Handling of Products and Ingredients

8. Use of Ingredients

9. Smoking

Chapter 5: Design Guidelines and Standards

Bakeries must comply with all local building and food preparation regulations. Best practice in food preparation design concerns the correct layout of equipments, sanitary facilities, waste facilities, storage, display and service as well as the selection and proper installation of specialized building materials such as tiling, resin or welded vinyl floors, sealed, washable wall claddings and fixed ceilings.

An environment that visibly supports hygienic food practices will encourage cleanliness from staff and provide for easier maintenance, improved ergonomics and productivity as well as reassuring potential customers.

1. Premises, Equipment and Vehicles

All bakery rooms shall be of a height adequate for proper ventilation. The walls and ceilings of preparation areas shall be constructed of a smooth material which is impervious to water and easily cleaned. Floors and walls shall fit tightly to prevent the accumulation of filth. Doors, windows, transoms, skylights and other openings shall be tightly screened between May first and November first of each year. The floors, walls and ceilings of each bakery, the equipment used in the handling or preparation of bakery products or the ingredients thereof, all vehicles transporting such products and the boxes, baskets and other receptacles in which such products are transported shall at all times be kept by the owner or operator of the bakery in a clean and sanitary condition and free from dirt and dust, flies, insects and other contaminating matter. All showcases, shelves and other places where bakery products are sold shall at all times be kept by the bakery well-covered, properly ventilated, adequately protected from dirt and dust, flies, insects and other contaminating matter, and in a sweet, clean and sanitary condition. Shipping baskets and other containers for transporting bakery products shall be kept clean.

2. Furniture, Utensils and Floor

Every room used for the manufacture of flour or meal food products shall have the furniture and utensils therein so arranged that they and the floor may at all times be kept clean and in good sanitary condition.

3. Cleanliness and Sanitation

Every bakery shall be constructed, drained, lighted, ventilated and maintained in a clean and sanitary condition, and screened against flies, shall have plumbing and drainage facilities, together with suitable wash basins, wash sinks and toilets or water closets, which shall be kept in a clean and sanitary condition. The said toilets or water closets shall be in rooms having no direct connection with any room in which bakery products or ingredients are prepared, stored, handled or displayed.

4. Sitting or Lounging Equipment

No person shall sit or lounge or be permitted to sit, lie or lounge upon any of the tables, shelves, boxes or other equipments or accessories used in connection with the production, preparation, packing, storing, display or sale of bakery products in a bakery.

5. Lighting and Safety Lighting

Lighting
For existing businesses without spatial separation of the bakery and the pastry/cake shop, the minimum requirement is 200 Lux.

If the mixing space, baking room and the workplace for decorating baked goods are separate, the following lighting strengths are required: Mixing space at least 300 Lux; Baking room at least 200 Lux; Work area for decoration at least 500 Lux.

If only the bakery and the pastry/cake shop are spatially separated: at least 300 Lux for the bakery; at least 500 Lux for the pastry/cake department with decorating workplaces.

If there is no spatial separation of the individual work areas: at least 300 Lux for the whole bakery.

Since there is increased contamination through flour dust, annual cleaning of the lighting installations is required.

Safety lighting
Safety lighting is required for the bakery and the escape routes. Storage areas and social areas should be equipped with escape route orientation lighting.

6. Wearing Apparel

In connection with every bakery, suitable room shall be provided for the changing and hanging of the wearing apparel of the workers or employees, which shall be separate and apart from the work, storage and sales rooms, and shall be kept in a clean and sanitary condition.

7. Keeping and Handling of Products and Ingredients

All bakery products and ingredients thereof shall be stored, handled, transported and kept so as to protect them from spoilage, contamination, disease and unwholesomeness. Boxes and other permanent receptacle or containers for the storing, receiving or handling of bakery products shall be so placed and constructed as to be beyond the reach of contamination from streets, alleys and sidewalks and from animals, and shall be kept clean and sanitary by the bakery.

clean and sanitary by the bakery.

8. Use of Ingredients

There shall not be used in bakery products or in the ingredients thereof any ingredient or material, including water, which is spoiled or contaminated or which may render the product unwholesome, unfit for food or injurious to health.

9. Smoking

Employees shall be prohibited from smoking while preparing and baking food products.

Index

71 ARQUITECTOS
Address: Av. Alexandre Herculano n.78
2900-206, Setubal, Portugal

a l m project
Address: 5544 Hollywood Boulevard Los Angeles CA 90028
Tel: +1 323 570 0571

Andrea Langhi Design
Tel: +393356462210

Architekt Jurgen Radatz
Address: 1130 Wien, Amalienstraße 6
Tel: 0699/11 45 48 94
Fax: 01/877 69 82

Bluarch Architecture + Interiors + Lighting
Address: 112 West 27th Street - Suite 302 - New York
New York 10001, USA
Tel: 212 929 5989
Fax: 212 656 1626

c3 Studio
Email: info@c3studio.ca

CASE-REAL
Address: 1-9-8 Imagawa Chuoh-ku Fukuoka 810-0054 Japan
Tel: +81 92 718 0770
Fax: +81 92 718 0777

Chrystalline Architect
Address: Taman Kebon jeruk intercon blok D1 no 12A
11630, West Jakarta, Jakarta Raya, Indonesia
Tel: +62 21 5890 4945

COLLIDANIELARCHITETTO
Address: Via Sannio 61 00183 Roma, Italy

Colli Galliano Architetti
Address: Via Napoli, 65 Rome in Italy
Tel: +39 06 48 91 30 87

Denis Kosutic

Address: Florianigasse 7/8 1080 Vieen, Austria
Tel: 43 699 19479990

Edha architects
Address: jl.pulau bira ll block c1 no. 19 taman permata buana
West Jakarta, Indonesia
Tel: +62 21 5826119

Forward Thinking Design
Address: Office 8, Suite 201, Lakeside Corporate Centre
29-31 Solent Circuit Baulkham Hills 2153
Tel: 02 8850 4977

Kois Associated Architects
Address:33 Vasileos Konstantinou Avene
10674, Athens, Attica, Greece

RAISERLOPES Architekten
Address: Hauptmannsreute 69 D - 70193 Stuttgart, Germany
Tel: +07 11 2 48 39 19 0
Fax: +07 11 2 48 39 19 99

Sandra Tarruella Interioristas
Address: Madrazo 83, Entl. 2a, 08006 Barcelona, Spain
Tel: +34 933 622 264

Studio Arihiro Miyake
Email: studio@arihiromiyake.com

Studio Guiseppe DondoniSGD
Address: Via del Fante, 13/D, 26013 Crema - Cremona, Italy
Tel: 038226946
Fax: 038226946

Studiounodesign Nuti & Bartolomeo
Address: SEDE OPERATIVA
Via Malaga, 4, 20143 - Milan, Italy

Surface3
Address: 305 Bellechase E, #208
Montreal (QC) Canda
Tel: + 1 514 270 8284
Fax: 1 514 270 8269

© 2013 by Design Media Publishing Limited
This edition published in Oct. 2013

Design Media Publishing Limited
20/F Manulife Tower
169 Electric Rd, North Point
Hong Kong
Tel: 00852-28672587
Fax: 00852-25050411
E-mail: suisusie@gmail.com
www.designmediahk.com

Editing: Vanessa Cullen
Proofreading: Chen Zhang
Design/Layout: Jie Zhou

All rights reserved. No part of this publication may be reproduced or transmitted in any form or by any means, electronic or mechanical, including photocopy, recording or any information storage and retrieval system, without prior permission in writing from the publisher.

ISBN 978-988-15662-2-5

Printed in China